Making every lesson count

Six principles to support great teaching and learning

Shaun Allison and Andy Tharby

Crown House Publishing Limited
www.crownhouse.co.uk

First published by

Crown House Publishing Limited
Crown Buildings, Bancyfelin, Carmarthen, Wales, SA33 5ND, UK
www.crownhouse.co.uk

and

Crown House Publishing Company LLC
PO Box 2223, Williston, VT 05495, USA
www.crownhousepublishing.com

First published 2015. Reprinted 2015 (twice), 2016 (twice), 2017.

The extract on page 70 is used with permission of Harry Fletcher-Wood. The strategy on pages 188–190 has been used with permission of David Brading. The activity on page 229 has been adapted with permission of Alex Quigley. The case study on pages 251–256 is used with permission of Dan Brinton. The case study on pages 257–259 is used with permission of Chris Hildrew. The case study on pages 259–262 is used with permission of Pete Jones. The case study on pages 262–263 is used with permission of Chris Woodcock.

Quotes from Ofsted documents used in this publication have been approved under an Open Government Licence. Please http://www.nationalarchives.gov.uk/doc/open-government-licence/version/3/.

British Library Cataloguing-in-Publication Data

A catalogue entry for this book is available from the British Library.

Print ISBN 978-184590973-4
Mobi ISBN 978-184590976-5
ePub ISBN 978-184590977-2
PDF ISBN 978-184590978-9

LCCN 2017942407

Printed and bound in the UK by
TJ International, Padstow, Cornwall

Foreword by Doug Lemov

A few years ago I spent a day touring schools in a major American school district. The district in question was committed to providing better training for its teachers. The organization that helped them design a summer training program to make sure newly qualified teachers were successful when they entered the classroom was using one of my books. The long tunnel of winter was turning to spring and things were going well. They invited me down to visit and see the results, and on the day in question we went from classroom to classroom to watch the new teachers at work.

Everything I'd read prior to my visit indicated that great things were afoot. The data on the new teachers indicated that they were proving more successful than almost any class of new teachers in the past – internal assessment data showed higher than expected student achievement levels; observations by school leaders were positive; the drop-out rate among the teachers low. This was all great news – the first years of teaching, in an urban school district in the US, can be brutal for new teachers. So brutal that The New Teacher Project, a highly respected organization here, found that about half of them quit in the first three years. But by every measure the district had, these teachers were surviving and thriving at higher rates than normal. The new teachers weren't perfect but they were on their way.

What I saw in classrooms that day unexpectedly eroded my optimism. It was plain to see that the teachers had developed a set of skills and that those skills were helpful to them in setting the conditions for learning. Students were engaged and ready to learn. There they were sitting brightly at their desks with their eyes up and alert and their minds ready. They wanted to learn; they appeared to like and trust their teachers. They were waiting, those students, for something great to happen. And that was the problem.

The lessons those bright-eyed, would-be scholars partici-pated in often lacked the fundamental elements of what a great lesson should look like. There was a general dearth of challenge and rigor. There wasn't much independent prac-tice. The goal seemed to be to keep students from getting turned off school by keeping them from struggling too much, so, for example, the texts they read were too easy. They read them; they were praised for reading them. But the intrinsic rewards that come from reading something rich and challenging were not bestowed upon those children. The end product did not push their minds. Other times they would do a handful of math problems say, but not fifteen of them of increasing challenge and complexity. And they rarely executed with autonomy. In the I/We/You model they did a lot of "I" (the teacher modeling) and "We" (guided practice) but not much "You" (independent practice).

It may have been better than what usually happened in a first year classroom, but it wasn't good enough. And often it wasn't the things the teachers hadn't thought of that betrayed their lessons but rather *the things they were trying to achieve.* They'd been *trained and socialized* (previous to attending the summer institute) to know not to give stu-dents text that was "too rigorous." They knew they should not give poor kids who might be behind in reading hard things to read. It's not that what they chose to read had not been given much thought but that it had that was so damning.

And the fact that their skills in some aspects of teaching had changed the culture among the children just made the need for rigor and challenge all the more urgent. The kids had done their part. They had bought in to the promise of "something more" but the something more wasn't "more" enough. To not deliver the kind of lessons that set their minds alight was to not deliver on a promise.

Let's be honest here. Skills matter. A lot. To walk into those classrooms with Dostoyevsky tucked under your arm but no

idea how to engage all kids, ask questions or establish order-
liness is to guarantee another, perhaps quicker and
occasionally spectacular, form of failure. But mastery of
skills without a clear vision of "what for" also isn't enough.

I holed up in my hotel room that night and into the wee
hours hammered out a note to my colleagues with thoughts
on how to develop a tool to help their trainees hold a vision
of what excellent and rigorous lessons looked like, as a constant lodestone and guide, even while they were learning the
fundamentals that would allow them to execute on that
vision fully somewhere down the road. I suggested something called a "rigor checklist" – basically a list of gut check
things teachers should be seeing and doing if they were on
the right track in terms of lesson design. It included things
like reading challenging text and doing lots of independent
writing in complete sentences followed by revision. If none
of the things on the list were happening regularly, it meant
there was probably a rigor problem. Skills must be developed
but without perspective and the right compass heading they
don't work that well.

If only Shaun Allison and Andy Tharby had written their
outstanding *Making Every Lesson Count* then it might have-
meant a less fraught and sleepless night for me and more
importantly better teaching for children in that city. Certainly
their document envisioning what a well-designed lesson
should encompass is better than what I put together in my
"checklist." Their book is not only immensely useful but a
great read – clear and thoughtful; direct and lively; written
– you will be reminded on almost every page – not by people
who sit in some theoretical aerie high above the fray but by
front line educators who live and breathe the fundamentals
of schooling every day in real schools with the full panoply
of challenges that implies.

Yes, I still believe teaching is a craft and that teachers succeed by refining their technique over and over, to better
execute the moments of their day, throughout their working

lives. Allison and Tharby do too I suspect. But what they provide in this book is a vision: what does the end product look like? What is it we're shooting for and why? What's most important? How do we avoid the burden of bad ideas in teaching? In particular their vision focuses on the centrality of challenge and the necessity of practice, the very two elements most likely to be missing from well-meaning lessons that just aren't rigorous enough. The very two things teachers were not providing to their eager students on that fateful day.

And of course while the visit to the schools I describe here reminds me how helpful it can be to early stage teachers, this book will be immensely useful to all teachers at all stages in their development. It's full of grounded and real world insight. I couldn't recommend it more highly.

Doug Lemov, managing director, Uncommon Schools, author of *Teach Like a Champion 2.0, Practice Perfect* and *Reading Reconsidered*

Acknowledgements

This book is dedicated to the fantastic teachers and students, past and present, whose work at Durrington High School continues to inspire and challenge us every single day. Without you to learn from, this book would simply not have been possible – so thank you. The recent rise of online teacher networks – through Twitter and blogging – has led us to engage with countless educators from across the globe, working in a wide range of contexts. You have broadened our horizons beyond all measure. Once again, our heartfelt thanks – we truly are standing on the shoulders of giants.

Shaun would like to say a special 'thank you' to the Senior Leadership Team at Durrington for your brilliant humour, support and unswerving commitment to excellence. You are an inspiration to me and I am lucky to work alongside you and learn from you. Above all though, I would like to thank my beautiful wife Lianne and my four gorgeous children, May, Finn, Eve and Jude. You are my world and I love you all very much.

Andy would like to pay special tribute to the English team at Durrington. Your good humour, decency and desire to do the best for our students have made for ten wonderful years. Mostly, though, I would like to thank Donna and George. Donna for your love, patience and for putting up with my infuriating absentmindedness during the writing of this book. And George for your indefatigable cheerfulness – you make me happy every day.

Contents

Introduction

One Easter, Shaun and his wife, Lianne, were clearing out their loft when they happened upon Lianne's dog-eared school books hidden away in a dark corner. They were from her fourth year (Year 10) chemistry lessons when she was taught by Mr Clarke, a teacher she remembers vividly to this day. They started to flick through. Her books were full of detailed, well-presented notes. Even thirty years later, Mr Clarke's teaching approach shone brightly from those dusty pages.

Chemistry was hugely challenging in Mr Clarke's lessons. In Year 2, Lianne was learning about valency; in Year 4, empirical formulae. As one of his students, it was your duty to raise your standards to meet his demands – he would never come down to meet you. Woe betide anybody whose efforts did not make the grade; Mr Clarke might publish your name on his infamous 'dirty dozen list'! You were always expected to respond to Mr Clarke's marking. He would write 'corrections' and you would be expected to repeat your incorrect answers until they were right. Mr Clarke did not worry about whether the work was intrinsically interesting. He cared that you learnt what you needed to know. Every student in Lianne's chemistry class achieved an O level grade C or above. And it was a mixed-ability group too.

Did Mr Clarke's lessons engage and motivate his students? You bet they did. He regularly won the school's 'teacher of the year' award and is still a local hero in Porthcawl, South Wales despite having retired some years ago. Lianne is now a successful science teacher.

As a profession we have become confused. After many years of educational research, nobody can put a definitive finger on what successful classroom practice really looks like. Yet teachers across centuries and millennia seemed to have managed perfectly well. Mr Clarke certainly did. Of course, successful teaching is more than a case of simply mimicking those we admire. We have to find something that works for us individually – in our classrooms, in our schools. Might it be, however, that in recent years the profession has so over-complicated definitions of 'good practice' that it has blinded itself from some simple truths?

Ofsted, who in the past have favoured and prescribed a preferred style of teaching, last year stepped back from grading individual lessons – instead letting schools define how successful teaching should look for themselves. In classrooms up and down Britain, teachers now have more freedom than they have had for a decade to develop and hone strategies that suit their preferred teaching style and the needs of their students. This is a welcome but daunting change. It also poses a question. If we are to make every lesson count, what simple and manageable actions have the greatest impact on learning?

We should categorically state from the outset that we do not believe in silver bullets. This book does not pretend to gift you with solid answers to every dilemma you will face. Instead, we offer a coherent ethos and six evidence-informed pedagogical principles that cut to the core of successful teaching: challenge, explanation, modelling, practice, feedback and questioning. We hope that the ideas we share will be useful to new and experienced teachers alike, as you look to further your understanding of how a rich climate for learning can be forged from the small details of practice.

Two values provide the bedrock for everything that follows in this book: *excellence* and *growth*. After reading Massachusetts middle-school teacher Ron Berger's wonderful book, *An Ethic of Excellence*,[1] we realised that in our headlong pursuit of fashionable pedagogical ideas – such as pace, rapid progress and independent learning – we had long neglected an eternal truth. That it is our fundamental responsibility to give children the chance to be excellent. Berger writes about how he immerses students in high standard exemplar work and models, allows them to redraft their work multiple times and builds up a culture of collegiate pride. The result is a culture of craftsmanship. All children, Berger argues, are apprentice craftsmen. They should be encouraged to hone and refine their work with pride and diligence until it reaches excellence.

But excellence is hard to come by. To achieve it, a child must work hard and be prepared to face the setbacks they will inevitably meet on the journey. This is where Stanford University psychologist Carol Dweck's ideas about mindset take centre stage. Dweck has found that human beings fall roughly into one of two broad categories: those who adopt a *fixed mindset* and those who adopt a *growth mindset*. Those who think in a fixed way believe that their ability is innate and cannot be changed: I was born clever – or stupid – and that way I will remain. Those alive to the possibility of growth, however, will attribute success or failure not to an unchangeable lack of ability, but to whether they have worked hard or not. Put simply, if a child flunks an exam there are two possible attributions they might make: place the blame on their natural ability and see no need to increase their effort next time around, or seek to learn from their mistakes with the aim to do better next time.

---

1 Ron Berger, *An Ethic of Excellence: Building a Culture of Craftsmanship with Students* (Portsmouth, NH: Heinemann, 2003).

Of course, it is the growth mindset that we must seek to encourage. Teachers and children need to realise, in Dweck's words, that 'working harder makes you smarter' and that it is old-fashioned effort that unlocks improvement, not a gift granted at birth. Dweck's research demonstrates that through the language we use with young people, adults can have a huge influence on the mindset a child adopts. How we frame success and failure, and the way we promote 'struggle' as a positive state, are hugely important. Viewed from another angle, Dweck's findings point at another principle behind this book: exemplary teachers are not born great, they *become* great.

Underpinning this book, then, are the notions gleaned from Dweck and Berger that expert teachers must be uncompromising in their quest to foster pride and hard work. Nevertheless, excellence and growth are soulless, vacuous aims without good teaching to bolster them. It means very little to ask a child to adopt this philosophy if we have not furnished them with the tools that make it possible. Indeed, Muijs and Reynolds conclude that research tends to show that 'the effect of achievement on self-concept is stronger than the effect of self-concept on achievement'.[2] In other words, teach students well and they will achieve; and if they achieve, they will begin to see themselves as successful learners. A school ethos of excellence and growth, then, can only truly be created through great teaching that leads to genuine learning.

An extensive report from the Sutton Trust entitled *What Makes Great Teaching?* argues that research evidence proves that many popular teaching practices are ineffective in improving student attainment.[3] The authors name the following strategies as being myths that have little impact on

---

2 Daniel Muijs and David Reynolds, *Effective Teaching: Evidence and Practice*, 3rd edn (London: Sage, 2011), p. 188.

3 Robert Coe, Cesare Aloisi, Steve Higgins and Lee Elliot Major, *What Makes Great Teaching? Review of the Underpinning Research* (London: Sutton Trust, 2014). Available at: http://www.suttontrust.com/wp-content/uploads/2014/10/What-makes-great-teaching-FINAL-4.11.14.pdf.

learning: lavishing low achieving students with praise; encouraging students to discover ideas for themselves; grouping by ability; rereading as a revision tool; attempting to improve motivation before teaching content; teaching to 'learning style'; and the idea that active learning helps you remember.

However, the two factors linked with the strongest student outcomes are:

♦ **Content knowledge**. Teachers with strong knowledge and understanding of their subject make a greater impact on students' learning. It is also important for teachers to understand how students think about content and be able to identify common misconceptions on a topic.

♦ **Quality of instruction**. This includes effective questioning and the use of assessment by teachers. Specific practices, like reviewing previous learning, providing model responses for students, giving adequate time for practice to embed skills securely and progressively introducing new learning (scaffolding) are also found to improve attainment.

It would be a mistake to adopt the broad brushstrokes of such findings crudely or uncritically. Our joint experiences have demonstrated again and again that schools should never underestimate the practical wisdom of the classroom teacher. Careful day-to-day decision-making, informed by years of thinking and practice, is vital. Situational factors have a huge influence too. Great teaching is not a single entity; it varies enormously from school to school, from subject to subject and from classroom to classroom. What makes you an exemplary practitioner in your environment might not make us exemplary teachers in ours – and vice versa. Needless to say, it would also be a grave mistake to dismiss the findings highlighted in the Sutton Trust report, and so the ideas shared in this book do lean on this and other sources of evidence, such as cognitive psychology.

It follows, then, that this book will combine three aspects when coming to a definition of effective teaching: what the research evidence suggests; what we have learnt from inspirational teaching colleagues at our school and in the burgeoning online education community; and, most of all, what we continue to learn from our day-to-day experiences as classroom teachers.

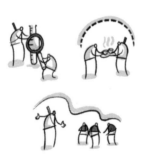

We have targeted six interrelated pedagogical principles. Inspired by the legendary rock band Led Zeppelin, ours is a 'tight but loose' approach. We have highlighted a few essentials to great teaching but leave you free to implement them and connect them as you see fit.

The principles work as follows:

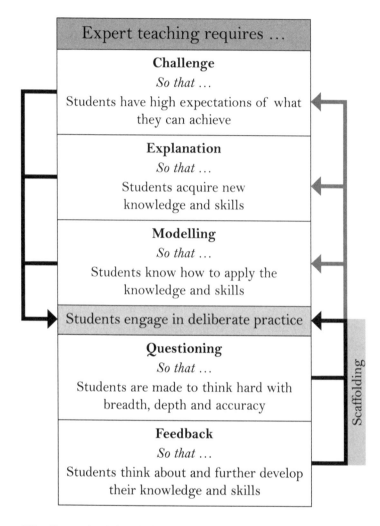

The first principle, *challenge*, is the driving force of teaching. Only by giving our students work that makes them struggle, and having the highest possible expectations of them, will we be able to move them beyond what they know and can do now. This will be the focus of Chapter 1.

Challenge informs teacher *explanation*, which is the skill of conveying new concepts and ideas. The trick is to make abstract, complex ideas clear and concrete in students' minds. It is deceptively hard to do well, and so we delve into the art and science of teacher talk in Chapter 2.

In Chapter 3 we move on to *modelling*. This involves 'walking' students through problems and procedures so that we can demonstrate the procedures and thought processes they will soon apply themselves. It also involves the use of exemplar work.

Without *practice* student learning will be patchy and insecure. They need to do it, and they need to do it many times as they move towards independence. In Chapter 4, we take heed of the findings from cognitive science research. It goes without saying that practice is the fulcrum around which the other five strategies turn. This is because it develops something that is fundamental to learning – memory.

Students need to know where they are going and how they are going to get there. Without *feedback*, our fifth principle and the subject of Chapter 5, practice becomes little more than 'task completion'. We give students feedback to guide them on the right path, and we receive feedback from students to modify our future practice. And so the cycle continues …

Chapter 6 leads us to our last principle – *questioning*. Like explanation, questioning is a skilful art. It has a range of purposes: it allows us to keep students on track by testing for misconceptions and it promotes deeper thought about subject content.

Finally, in Chapter 7, we consider how school leaders can put structures and systems in place that will allow a climate of excellence and growth to take root and flourish. We include a number of case studies, including from some of the most influential school leaders in the UK.

Through the application of these six principles, the ultimate goal is to lead students towards independence. The idea of 'independent learning' is often misunderstood. Independence is a desirable outcome of teaching, not a teaching strategy in its own right. Our job is to teach children, rather than to cross our fingers in the hope they will learn on their own. Classroom management and relationships are of great importance too, yet they are not the subject of this book. Without a strong classroom climate in place, it is unlikely that the above principles will have much effect. Even so, research shows that sometimes, even if a child is working hard and engaged, new learning might not be taking place.[4]

So, how do these six principles relate to one another? Well, to be clear, this is not a neat cycle to be adhered to in every lesson. Learning is highly complex. It ebbs and flows through lessons, across schemes of work and over years. In fact, the hackneyed 'three-part' lesson of starter, main and plenary is hopelessly simplistic. Some learning cycles are simple, quick and over in minutes. Others are much longer loops covering two, three or more lessons. Others still are choppy and messy, returning back to teacher explanation and modelling repeatedly as students struggle to refine new knowledge and skill through lots of practice and focused feedback. Some sequences will prove so simple and quick that all six principles will be unnecessary. Others will require them all.

To explain to a child how to spell 'accommodation' might take a matter of minutes – 'Two cots need two mattresses in any accommodation!' – plus a bit of practice using the word in context. To teach the same child how to write a speech, however, will require a more comprehensive sequence. You will set the level of challenge high by introducing students to seminal historical speeches – those by Elizabeth I, Winston Churchill and Martin Luther King, perhaps. These will act as exemplars to inspire their own writing, but you

---

4   Graham Nuthall, *The Hidden Lives of Learners* (Wellington: New Zealand Council for Educational Research Press, 2007), p. 24.

will also need to model explicitly some key aspects of speech-writing with the class: an arresting opening, a well-evidenced argument, a powerful ending. Students will need to practise these discrete features and receive feedback on their performance before they embark on writing a full speech of their own. Perhaps they will redraft as a result of your feedback. Through each stage of the unit of work, you will have questioned them to find out what they understand and to provoke deeper thinking.

The majority of this book is dedicated to sharing the planning, delivery and assessment strategies that bring each of the six principles to life. For instance, there are ten strategies to accompany Chapter 4 on practice, including The Power of Three on the importance of repetition, Fold It In on building regular practice of important concepts into long-term planning, and Pair Their Writing, a strategy that involves students verbally supporting one another during writing practice. Each chapter begins with two typical classroom scenarios. These are fictional but rooted in problems we and many other teachers encounter on a daily basis.

Our hope is that you will pick and choose from the strategies as you see fit. While one teacher might use all the strategies with great success, the next might have little success with any of them. What matters most is how and why they are implemented. They will need to be adapted and refined to suit the content you are teaching and the children you are teaching it to.

We propose that all planning should start with the question: what is the subject content I aim to teach to the students in front of me? It is at this point that the principles and their supporting strategies come into play. We suggest that you adopt the individual strategies as rough ideas to adjust, modify and combine to suit your subject and teaching style. Aim to capture their essence, their spirit, rather than to apply them as hard-and-fast rules. Ours is not a regimented, thought-free approach to teaching.

A persuasive line of argument suggests that generic teaching strategies, such as those we share in this book, are a distraction; that pedagogy is more effective when it is subject specific. In general we agree: delivery of subject content must be the primary concern. However, there are some fundamentals to teaching and learning that we should all be made aware of. This is why each chapter starts with a description of the principle and why it works, and then moves on to practical strategies. Once you understand the essential concept you can decide which strategies can be usefully adapted for your subject.

We hope you will enjoy our book and be as inspired in the reading of it as we have been by the teaching that has inspired it. Most of all, we hope that you will relish building and maintaining a culture of growth and excellence with your students. Teachers like Mr Clarke are certainly not relics from a bygone era.

challenge

explanation

modelling

DELIBERATE PRACTICE

feedback

Questioning

scaffolding

Chapter 1
Challenge

Evie

Evie arrives at secondary school with the label 'less able'. She has fallen behind during her primary years in the basics – reading, writing and arithmetic. She is a hard-working, conscientious child from an underprivileged background. She receives little support from home. On arrival at secondary school, Evie takes a number of baseline tests and before long finds herself in the bottom set for many subjects. In unstreamed subjects, teachers differentiate by giving her easier work to complete than her peers. Teachers rarely expect more than this from Evie – after all, somebody has to be the weakest in the group. It is no wonder then that Evie herself has little expectation that she can become an academic achiever. After five years of secondary school, Evie enters the real world. She has failed her GCSEs.

Emma, the English NQT

During her first year as an English teacher, Emma decides to take a risk and teach a poem she has always loved to her Year 9 group, Robert Browning's 'Porphyria's Lover'. It is a sullen

Thursday afternoon in late November and the lesson is noth-
ing short of a disaster. The classroom is awash with cries of
'I don't get it', 'Why do we have to do poetry?' and 'Mr
Brown's class next door are watching a video today.' At last
the bell rings for the end of the day, and Emma vows never
again to attempt Browning with her Year 9 groups. She will
look for an easier alternative next year.

Challenge –
What It Is And Why It Matters

Put simply, challenge in education is the provision of difficult work that causes students to think deeply and engage in
healthy struggle. It is unfortunate that all too often challenge is presented in the context of 'challenging the most
able'. Evie's story is an extreme logical extension of this
phenomenon. Teachers were only ever expected to support
her, never challenge her. Sadly, these low expectations, consciously and subconsciously, were transferred to Evie herself,
whose schooling became defined by a lack of self-belief.
Fascinating, if controversial, research from Rosenthal and
Jacobson in the 1960s, into what they dubbed 'the Pygmalion
effect', suggests that our expectations of students can have
a profound effect not only on how we interact with them but
also on the student's future achievement.[1] They found – and
it makes for uncomfortable reading – that teachers in their
study would interact differently with those students of
whom they had higher expectations. They would be 'warmer'
towards these children, teach them more material, give them
more time to respond to questions and provide them with
more positive praise.

---

1 For more on the Pygmalion effect, see Philip Zimbardo, The Pygmalion Effect
   and the Power of Positive Expectations [video] (25 September 2011).
   Available at: http://www.youtube.com/watch?v=hTghEXKNj7g.

It is bizarre, morally questionable even, that we have come to believe that only those we describe as the 'most able' need or deserve to be challenged. Some overarching principles are needed to help us to use challenge in the classroom:

♦ It is not just about the 'most able'.

♦ We should have high expectations of all students, all the time.

♦ It is good for students to struggle just outside of their comfort zone, as that is when they are likely to learn most.

The first and last points relate to Carol Dweck's work on mindsets. Those students who adopt a growth mindset are more likely to understand that hard work, effort and learning from failure are vital to their future success. Providing them with challenging work is easy for the teacher; they are likely to embrace it. They will enjoy the struggle and see this as integral to their learning. It is the underachieving, fixed mindset students that cause us most difficulty. To them, effort feels fruitless and seems to compound their negative self-perception. Because they want to be seen as bright at all costs, they do not want to be considered as struggling. The temptation, as a teacher, is to give these students 'easy work' for a quiet life. Because the work leads to no real effort or deep thinking, it is very unlikely that they are learning. However, it keeps them satisfied because by completing the work they will not have to lose face through public failure.

Instead, we need to move these students from a fixed to a growth mindset, and the only way to do this is to give them more challenging work and to support them by helping them to believe that they can do it. We want to shift them to a position where, through hard work, resilience and determination, they will eventually embrace the struggle.

Have you ever been told, following a lesson observation, that your lesson was 'badly pitched' because students were struggling? This is an odd statement because, within reason, struggle supports learning. A careful balance needs to be struck – as in the figure below. While we want to move students out of their comfort zone into the struggle zone, we also need to ensure that we do not push them too far so that they end up in the panic zone. Hattie and Yates have summarised research showing that useful learning will not occur when there is too much new material for our working memory – the part of the mind responsible for holding and processing information – to cope with.[2] The skill of the effective teacher, therefore, is to push students just far enough so that they are in a productive struggle, but not so far that they drown in a sea of panic.

Comfort zone	Struggle zone	Panic zone

Low challenge. Low stress. Limited thinking. Limited learning.	High challenge. Low stress. Thinking required. Effective learning.	Very high challenge. High stress. Cognitive overload. Limited learning.

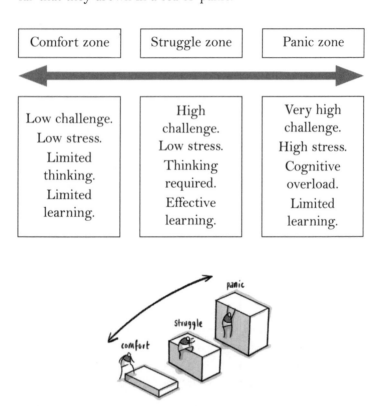

2 John Hattie and Gregory Yates, *Visible Learning and the Science of How We Learn* (Abingdon: Routledge, 2014), pp. 149–152.

The second scenario at the beginning of this chapter featured Emma, the NQT English teacher, grappling to teach a difficult poem to an uncooperative class. The students were possibly experiencing cognitive overload or perhaps feigning laziness. The solution here is to reconsider how to teach the poem, rather than to scrap it from the curriculum forever. If ample time is given to teaching the poem step by step, then teaching 'Porphyria's Lover' to the full ability range is eminently possible. The take-away here is that *challenge must start at home* – with us, the teachers.

So where does this leave differentiation, which is conventionally thought of as the teacher providing students of different abilities with work to match their 'ability profile'? The figure below demonstrates our solution to the problem of ensuring that needs are met, yet keeping the challenge high.

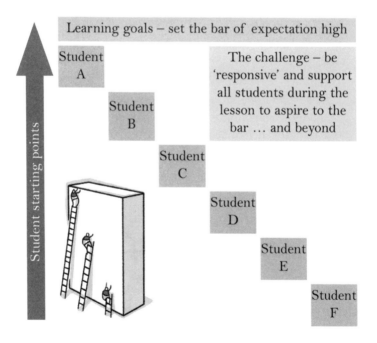

This model suggests that we should set the bar of expectation high for all students, irrespective of their starting points. Our job, then, is to respond to and support students during lessons, and over weeks, months and years, so that they all strive to reach, or in some cases surpass, this common goal. In doing so, differentiation will lie in the skilfulness of our response to the anticipated and unanticipated difficulties that our students will encounter along the way. This can only work effectively if we understand the individual students we are teaching, we have a deep knowledge of subject content and we know which parts of our subject students tend to find difficult.

For example, imagine your students are writing an essay on Shylock from Shakespeare's *The Merchant of Venice*. They are five minutes into the task when ...

♦ Callum puts his hand up and asks how to spell 'traumatised', as he often does with new vocabulary. You tap the dictionary on his desk and smile, but repeat the word for the whole class to reinforce your expectation that students employ challenging vocabulary.

♦ Grace's hand shoots up. You smile and motion it down. She smiles wryly back, sensing that, once again, you are encouraging her to be more resilient.

♦ 'Less able' Katy has not written a thing. You verbalise the first half of a sentence and she finishes it. Then she writes it down and off she goes.

♦ You and your teaching assistant circulate for a couple of minutes armed with highlighter pens. You randomly zoom in on students who are likely to have misspelled words and either highlight them or put a dot in the margin for the student to work out where the mistake is.

♦ On your rounds, you have noticed the clunky overuse of 'this' at the start of sentences. You stop the class and explain how they can use 'which' clauses (relative clauses) to combine sentences into fluent complex sentences.

- You come to Matt, incredibly able but prone to prolixity. He must cut out ten unnecessary words before continuing.

- Graham has written a page and a half of scrawled nonsense and is swinging back in his chair. You hand him a piece of paper and tell him to redraft the first paragraph, this time using the paragraph structure you have given him. You sense potential defiance and remind him that it is breaktime after the lesson.

In this scenario, all the students are given the same task, yet your response to individuals is different. These responses are decided not according to preconceived assumptions of need, but to genuine needs as they arise. High expectations are in place because you set the bar high to start with. You then differentiate downwards as you experiment with the most suitable strategy to hoist each individual child up. This is a highly subtle skill that takes many years to learn. You will never master it fully – no two children are quite the same!

We believe that much that is promoted as good differentiation practice is both unmanageable and counterproductive: it is not humanly possible to personalise planning for each and every child, nor, as often suggested, is it possible to create three levels of worksheet for every lesson.

The following strategies provide you with some simple, transferable ideas to help you challenge your students – and yourself.

1. Make Them Single and Challenging

How can I prepare lessons that challenge every student?

In recent years, there has been a trend to use *all*, *most* and *some* learning objectives at the start of lessons to cater for differing student entry points. Take this example from a biology lesson on photosynthesis:

All students will describe the factors required for photosynthesis.

Most students will be able to write a word equation for photosynthesis.

Some students will be able to write a balanced formula equation for photosynthesis.

What message does this give to students? As long as I can reach the first objective, I have done enough? Why risk failure and humiliation in front of my peers by attempting the other ones and getting them wrong? Through this method we may well be perpetuating low expectations.

A single, challenging learning objective is a far more aspirational:

Describe and explain the process and chemical nature of photosynthesis.

As a result, our expectations remain high for all, whatever their starting point. The role of the teacher, then, is to support all to reach, or even go beyond, this point. Naturally, not all will always get there, so our next job will be to work out an alternative approach for these students. Consider the fact that many of the students we categorise as 'low ability', like Evie, may never have been required to meet a challenging learning objective over many years of schooling. Is it any wonder that these children typically make very little progress?

2. Scale Up

How do I gauge whether lesson content is challenging or not?

A rule of thumb is to take into account the expected knowledge, concepts and skills in your subject and teach your classes just beyond that point. So at Key Stage 3, for example, dip into GCSE level; at GCSE, dip into A level; at A level, dip into undergraduate work. In doing so, the most challenging concepts that the assessment criteria require them to know will not be the most challenging topics they will have been exposed to. In fact, we have found that students find it very motivating to be told that they are studying something intrinsically difficult.

One of the most robust findings in experimental psychology is that of the *anchor effect*. Our perceptions, whether we consciously realise it or not, are unduly influenced by the first piece of information we receive on a topic – the anchor, if you like.[3] Imagine you are bartering for a porcelain jug at your local car-boot fair. When you hear from the seller that the price is £100, all negotiations are adjusted up and down from that figure – £55 suddenly sounds like a bargain, even if the jug is actually worth mere pennies.

This works as a useful metaphor for how we should plan for challenge in our classrooms. By exposing students to content at a level usually considered above (or beyond) national expectations, we anchor in challenge. Success is measured by adjusting up and down from here. This also works for the start of lessons. As soon as the students cross the threshold, they should be challenged to think about the topic at hand. For example: What does this picture tell you about ...? Write down five things you know about ...

If the anchor is set too low so that the content of lessons is less stretching, then, needless to say, overall success will be adjusted up or down from this inferior position. Therefore, if we are to genuinely challenge our students, we must take on the guise of the unscrupulous car-boot seller. Set our original price high and we are more likely to achieve better results than if we set it low. So, for example, introduce GCSE English literature students to the basics of feminist and Marxist critical theory, or in science, when teaching enzyme action and denaturation, explain the intermolecular forces that hold the active site in shape and how this changes as a result of increased temperature.

Critical to the success of this strategy is that not only do you set high expectations, but you also make students aware that you are doing so: 'Today, Year 7 we are doing GCSE standard work!' You are introducing challenging content

---

3   Daniel Kahneman, *Thinking, Fast and Slow* [Kindle edn] (London: Allen Lane, 2011), loc. 1998–2180.

because you have the highest expectations of them and the faith that they will be successful. But you will need to couch your language carefully – you want to inspire, not overwhelm.

While many students may not grasp these tough concepts at first, with time and patience they will get there. In *Switch*, Chip and Dan Heath write of 'destination postcards': the crystal-clear, long-term goals we must help our students to imagine and strive towards.[4] It is important, however, to remember that they will need to be guided towards these challenging targets in simple, manageable stages, otherwise they will quickly become lost and frustrated (this is an idea we extend in The Long Haul on page 35).

Individual starting points we cannot change; it is the destinations we need to scale up.

3. Know Thy Subject

How can I improve my subject knowledge and ensure that students are thinking deeply about it?

If you are going to stretch and challenge all students, be careful not to neglect your own subject knowledge. Indeed, research demonstrates that a deficit in teacher subject knowledge can be a barrier to student achievement.[5] So, keep up to date with subject-specific journals, websites and research papers, and keep abreast of the latest research findings in your subject area in the media. Resolve to read five books a year that will enhance and add extra texture to your

---

4 Chip Heath and Dan Heath, *Switch: How To Change Things When Change Is Hard* (London: Random House, 2011).
5 Coe et al., *What Makes Great Teaching?*, p. 2.

subject understanding. Go to the theatre, visit art galleries, subscribe to *New Scientist* or *National Geographic* or watch world-beating athletes in action. A history teacher could read a new biography of Hitler before teaching a unit on the First World War; a geography teacher could watch a series of documentaries on the 2004 Asian tsunami before teaching the topic.

As busy professionals we cannot read around every new topic, but the cumulative effect of a little reading over the years will have a slow but impressive impact. School leaders and subject leaders should also consider putting in place subject content continuing professional development (CPD), as we have at our school. One teacher reads up on a difficult topic, road-tests some ideas in the classroom and then shares the findings with the rest of the department. It is particularly fruitful to focus on common student misconceptions and how to tackle them head on.

A great exercise is to regularly answer challenging exam questions in your subject area and then ask for feedback from a trusted colleague on your performance. Compare your answers to the standard required for an A*. If your work does not meet the standard, why not? What valuable teaching points can you take from this? It is more than likely that you have struggled in the places that your students will struggle too.

Similarly, we should also challenge students to think about subject content. In *Why Don't Students Like School?*, cognitive scientist Daniel Willingham argues that 'memory is the residue of thought'.[6] In other words, we remember what we think about. Challenges should ensure that students are primarily thinking about subject content because, if not, they may remember something very different from that you intended. For instance, your history students might be completing a difficult task, such as writing a rhyming poem

---

6   Daniel T. Willingham, *Why Don't Students Like School?: A Cognitive Scientist Answers Questions About How the Mind Works and What It Means for the Classroom* (San Francisco, CA: Jossey-Bass, 2009), p. 54.

about life in the trenches during the First World War or completing a presentation on the Tudors using a new high-tech software package. However, if these 'challenges' mean that students have spent most of their time thinking about rhyming schemes or how to add animations to a slide-show, they will not have spent time thinking about the historical content you need them to learn and remember. Challenges should be firmly rooted in subject content.

4. Share Excellence

How can I ensure that my classroom and school environment promote excellence and challenge?

Festooned with bubble writing and pretty pictures, classroom displays often consist of attractive posters which bear little relation to the assessment mechanisms of the subject. So, why not use the display space in your classroom to show an enlarged version of an excellent written response to a challenging question in your subject? This sets the standard of expectation high and gives you something to refer to when describing what excellence looks like in your subject. It is hard for students to aspire to excellence if they have no inkling of what it looks like.

Art departments tend to be fantastic at this. To walk into the classroom of a great art teacher is to be surrounded by examples of excellent student work. Everywhere. What a hugely encouraging message this gives to students.

◆ This is what excellence looks like.

◆ This is the standard I expect you to replicate.

◆ Study it closely and you will see why it's excellent.

Why, then, is this not replicated in other subjects? There is every reason to display an excellent history essay on your wall, annotated to highlight how it meets and surpasses the success criteria, a write-up of a scientific experiment or a particularly complicated mathematical problem.

This can be replicated at a department or whole-school level. Take an area of your school and transform it into a Gallery of Excellence like the one below. (This idea was inspired by Pete Jones of Les Quennevais School, Jersey, who has written a case study for Chapter 7.)

By mounting the work in frames and displaying it in a prominent place, you are making a statement about your values:

♦ You have high expectations of what students can achieve and expect them to be inspired by the success of others.

♦ You accept that hard work and effort are needed to master new ideas and achieve excellence.

♦ You accept that students need to be resilient and keep going when things get tough.

♦ You promote the idea of excellence as the status quo.

Once established, there are a number of ways in which a gallery like this can be used:

♦ Subject exhibitions. Over the course of a year, each subject is allocated a time slot when they are expected to display examples of excellent work from their curriculum area. This also facilitates gallery critique (see Open a Gallery in Chapter 5). Classes are taken on a trip to the gallery for a lesson to admire, analyse and critique the work. The visit then inspires subsequent student work.

◆ Aiding transition. Before students join our school, we ask their primary schools for examples of excellent work. By displaying these in the gallery in September, when they start with us, they are immediately made to feel a part of the school community and reminded of the standard we expect them to build on.

◆ Public viewings. Invite school governors and parents to viewings of the gallery after school. This gives parents a concrete example of the standard of excellence to aim for so they know what to expect of their children and can discuss this with them at home.

5. Unstick Them

How do I support students when they are struggling with challenging tasks?

Skilled teachers know how long to let their students struggle for before intervening. It becomes like a sixth sense and develops with practice and experience. There are many instances when, if your students cannot do something, they will require your help. Having let them struggle for a while, it is time to give them the answer and teach them the strategy they need to get there. Next time, they will have an idea about what to do when they don't know what to do.

This relates to the idea of surface and deep learning, as advocated by John Hattie.[7] Simply speaking, *surface learning* refers to knowing the 'facts' about a topic, whereas *deep learning* refers to how we are able to relate, link and extend this knowledge. The most skilled teachers are able to judge perfectly how much time to spend on surface learning before moving on to deep learning. Problems may arise when too much time (or not enough time) is spent on surface learning before moving on to deep learning.

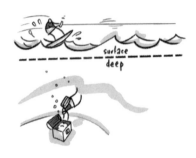

For example, a history class might be writing an essay exploring and evaluating the events that led up to the Reformation. It might become clear to the teacher that student knowledge about the chronology of the main events is not as secure as it needs to be in order to write the essay well. In this instance, the teaching skill is to stop and unstick them by explaining the events again, or reminding them where to find the information, before returning to the evaluation work.

A contrasting situation might occur in an English lesson when students are studying a novel and looking at the author's use of characterisation. Students may have spent so long finding relevant facts and quotations that the teacher has not moved them on to considering more interesting

---

7   John Hattie, The Science of Learning, keynote speech presented at OSIRIS World-Class Schools Convention, London, 2014. There is a write-up of the event at: http://classteaching.wordpress. com/2014/05/19/a-grand-day-out-with-hattie-waters/.

ways of interpreting the character's motivations and role in the story. As a result of a lack of extension, students' understanding remains at a simplistic level lacking in depth.

Maintaining a high level of challenge, therefore, is not simply about ploughing on with difficult content regardless. It is about making subtle adjustment after subtle adjustment so that students are not only exposed to new content but they also learn it securely and, with time, extend on it too.

6. Layer Their Writing

What simple, practical strategies can be put in place to challenge students to produce better writing?

Too often we ask students to produce a piece of writing and we accept their first attempt. In fact, we should insist that through effort and determination students produce work that they are rightly proud of. Truly high quality work requires thought, reflection and redrafting. This redrafting process needs careful structure and support. Both of us have really taken to redrafting in our lessons over recent years and have seen the quick, positive effects it can have. However, without clear guidance a redrafted piece of work can become little more than a painstakingly tidy version of the original.

Layered writing, developed by our former colleague, English teacher Gavin McCusker, provides a useful structure for redrafting in any subject area. The inspiration comes from the great artists who develop masterpieces by building their work up in layers. Each layer slowly increases the subtlety and texture of the painting. The same approach can be applied to writing. Having written the first draft of an analytical essay, a 'writer's palette' can be introduced to scaffold and extend students' ideas, as in the English example on pages 31–32.

Students then check through their work crossing off the analytical words and phrases they have used. Following this, they redraft their work, using more of the words and phrases as necessary to add depth and complexity to their writing.

This type of grid can be easily adapted to suit the needs of any subject. This is just one strategy we have seen that successfully supports redrafting, but there are plenty of others (see Chapter 5). Redrafting strategies like this one are useful because:

♦ They challenge students to strive for excellence – if it's not excellent, it's not finished!

♦ They encourage students to carefully reread and critique their own work.

♦ They build students' pride in their excellent work which they are then more likely to want to share with their peers.

Some teachers are rightly concerned that redrafting takes away vital time from teaching subject content. However, one of the reasons that bad writing habits become engrained and seemingly intractable is that students are rarely given the time to work on their mistakes. Redrafting allows for this.

Deep language analysis – writer's palette

Use a quote	Use speech marks	Embed quotes	Use an adjective in your explanation	Use a verb in your explanation	Use an adverb in your explanation	Explain the effect of a single word in LOTS of detail
Explain the effect of a verb	Explain the effect of an adverb	Explain the effect of an adjective	Explain the effect of a metaphor	Explain the effect of a simile	Explain the effect of alliteration	Explain the effect of onomatopoeia
Explain the effect of oxymoron	Explain the effect of hyperbole	Explain the effect of personification	Make another suggestion on the same quote	Make connections between the writer's language choices	Make connections between the writer's language devices	Use new words from a thesaurus in your analysis

Write 'this suggests'	Write 'this highlights'	Write 'this implies'	Write 'this reinforces'	Write 'this emphasises'	Write 'this further emphasises'	Write 'this intimates'
Explain the overall effect of the piece because of the writer's language choices	**Starter sentence:** One of the first powerful moments in the poem/novel/play/extract is …	**Starter sentence:** While on the surface … underneath	**Starter sentence:** Despite …	**Starter sentence:** Although …	**Starter sentence:** Even though …	**Starter sentence:** Throughout the poem/novel/play/extract …
Starter sentence: To emphasise a sense of … the writer	**Starter sentence:** To reinforce a sense of …	**Starter sentence:** On the one hand … yet on the other …	**Starter sentence:** In some ways …	**Starter sentence:** Not only … but …	**Starter sentence:** The poem/novel/play questions the idea of …	**Starter sentence:** The most interesting thing about …

7. Benchmark Brilliance

How do I ensure that challenge becomes the status quo in my lessons?

When our students arrive with us in secondary school, they tend to embark on a series of tests known as 'baseline assessments'. Invariably, these are tasks for which there is little or no preparation. More often than not, students flunk them: nerves, lack of practice and uncertainty about expectations all play a part. The danger is that, for some, this poor quality becomes a self-fulfilling general standard.

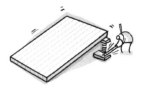

Thankfully there is another way. With a few nudges in the right direction at this critical point, we can help students to reshape their image of themselves as learners. We should ask students, fresh in the honeymoon glow of a move to secondary school, to do something that truly challenges them. The idea is that in every subject students undertake a task, complete a procedure, interrogate an idea or create a product that takes them far beyond the shackles of what they believe themselves to be capable of.

Before embarking on this task, consider these two questions:

♦ How will I plan a sequence of lessons that helps me to bleed the absolute best out of my students?

♦ How will I get them to invest in the task so that they really do care about the final product?

The following sequence provides a useful framework for students to produce a benchmark of brilliance in your subject.

1   Think about the task you are going to give the students to do. It needs to be something that will result in an end product, such as a piece of poetry or fictional writing, a write-up of a science experiment, a mathematical problem, a painting, a historical essay and so on. A rule of thumb should be that you expect students to complete a piece at GCSE level, as we suggested in the Scale Up strategy.

2   Show students examples of excellent finished pieces of work – if possible, more than one.

3   Deconstruct this work together. What are the features that make it so good? How would they start a piece of work like this? What key terms and phrases have been used? What thought processes and stages might they have gone through to get here? Naturally, the emphasis will be different depending on your subject, but be sure to take time with this – it is the most crucial stage. Having a large version of the work available that you can annotate as a class is a great idea. (See Chapter 3 for more ideas on the modelling and deconstruction process.)

4   Before they embark on their own piece of work, make sure that structures and scaffolds are available, such as key words, sentence starters, paragraph headings, section titles and worked examples.

5   As they are working, identify some of the strongest pieces, take a photograph and share it with the class. This will give you the opportunity to engage the class with some peer critique. The following questions are useful: What is good about the piece of work? How does it compare to the example that we deconstructed at the start of the lesson/sequence of work? How could it be improved? What would you add to it? How will you

improve your own piece on the basis of our critique of this example?

6   Ensure that students proofread and hand in their first draft to you for some personalised, written feedback to act on in the next lesson.

7   Ask them to carefully redraft in the next lesson.

Andy used the above sequence with Year 8 students to challenge them to 'write like Jack London'. Using extracts from *White Fang* as models, his students looked closely at London's descriptive style. Slowly and carefully, with suggested vocabulary and sentence structures, the students wrote their own pieces. They redrafted following feedback and each student produced one or two sides of vivid, atmospheric descriptive writing. The last part of the process was to celebrate the work. Each final piece was attached to the student's folder as a reminder of what they should expect from themselves in the future. The hard work, diligence and final products were astonishing.

8. The Long Haul

How do I embed challenge in the long term?

It is a misunderstanding to consider challenge just in terms of individual lessons. In reality these are only stepping stones to longer term goals, which is where the true challenge must lie. The long-term goals of elite sportsmen and women provide a useful comparison – for instance, winning a gold medal at the Olympics or playing in the Champions League. Training schedules will involve a slow and methodical build-up towards these aspirations, based around refining their skills bit by bit after regular and precise feedback.

Lessons should be considered in a similar way – as building blocks towards medium and long-term aims. Often lesson plans will need to be torn up and different routes will need to be forged. As long as we keep the destination in mind (e.g. to be able to solve quadratic equations, to serve a tennis ball successfully, to write a formal speech), how they get there and how quickly they get there become of less importance. Regular, rigorous and built-in assessment plays a crucial role in providing the structure for these goals.

Too easily, we can become obsessed with the details of individual lessons when in fact they are only parts of a greater whole. Challenge, therefore, is about having a clear but realistic vision about where our students need to go – along with helping them to share that vision with us. To make this happen, we need to be forward-thinking and unrelenting.

So what can we do to support this?

Simply telling students to aim for a 'grade A' is all but useless. They need concrete examples. So, as soon as they enter the classroom, immerse them in examples of excellence (as we suggested in Share Excellence). Textiles teacher Steve Bloomer does this brilliantly in his room. Examples of excellence are hanging from the ceiling so that students, when they might be struggling to simply stitch together two pieces of fabric, cannot help but see the overall goal they are eventually aiming for.

Here are some ways to implement The Long Haul:

1   At the start of the course, get students to write a letter to themselves from the perspective of their future self, looking back having finished the course. Why were they so successful? What did they do every lesson that enabled them to achieve their overall goal?

2   Keep referring forward. During lessons, when students successfully master a particular skill or area of knowledge, tell them how that will help them to achieve their long-term goal. In science you might say: 'It's great that you can now describe the steps involved in the process of genetic engineering as this will enable you to answer the six mark extended writing question in your exam.' In English this might be: 'Now that you can vary sentence lengths and structures to create tension, next you can combine these skills in the opening paragraph of your Gothic horror story.'

3   Rather than relying on our feedback, regularly ask students to reflect on their perceptions of their own performance. For example: 'Do you think that this piece of work is as good as you can make it? Is it going to allow you to meet your own goals? If not, what else do you need to do in order to improve it?' Of course, if we

notice that a student has low expectations we will need to intervene to help to raise them.

4   Use a sticker like the one below on the front of exercise books and folders so that students can keep a running record of their progress.

In this subject I am aiming for a grade ___.
In order to achieve this, I will need to ensure that I:

This can be added to as the course progresses, but they have ownership of it. It will help them to visualise how every lesson builds towards their overall goal, which in this case is a successful GCSE grade.

9. Plan for Progression

How do we ensure that we systematically build up student knowledge and skill?

Our planning should ensure that we think about how we will scale up the learning over a period of time. This will vary from subject to subject, but SOLO (Structure of Observed Learning Outcomes) taxonomy provides a good framework for planning for increased complexity in learning.[8]

---

8   See John Biggs and Kevin Collis, *Evaluating the Quality of Learning: The SOLO Taxonomy* (New York: Academic Press, 1982).

	Level of learning	SOLO taxonomy	What it means?
Excellence	**Deep**	Extended Abstract	Can extend and apply ideas. Extended thinking.
Secure		Relational	Can link and relate ideas. Strategies for thinking and reasoning.
Developing	**Surface**	Multistructural	Many ideas. Basic skills and concepts.
Foundation		Unistructural	Single idea. Recall and reproduction.

To initially secure surface learning, students need to go from knowing a single fact about a topic to knowing multiple facts – that is, going from unistructural to multistructural. In biology, for example, they may start by knowing that plants need light to live (unistructural). This idea can then be developed with more facts (multistructural): plants need light, water and carbon dioxide to thrive. In order to move this towards deep learning, they will need to be able to link these ideas together (relational) – in this case, they will need to understand that light provides the energy to convert water and carbon dioxide into glucose and oxygen. Developing this idea further (extended abstract), will require them to consider the interplay between photosynthesis and other chemical reactions, such as factors affecting the rate of photosynthesis.

While there is much discussion about the suitability of SOLO as a tool for students, it can provide a useful framework for planning lessons in a number of subjects. However, it is not necessarily applicable to every subject area. It is just another way to conceptualise the transition between surface and deep learning. We provide an explanation of how SOLO can be used to support assessment without levels in the Durrington High School case study in Chapter 7.

So, how can we plan for the transition between surface learning and deep learning?

♦ Use hinge questions to ascertain whether students have the key knowledge before progressing to the deeper learning (see Chapter 6 on questioning).

♦ Always have some planned 'extender' tasks for students to deepen their learning. These could be based on the principles of SOLO taxonomy, but they don't have to be. The expectation should be that anyone, irrespective of ability, can go on to the extender task. Here is a science example:

Dissolving it

NaCl crystal structure   NaCl in water

   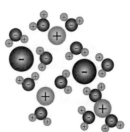

Sodium (Na) Chlorine (Cl)

What is happening here?
Why would this then conduct electricity?

Extenders
What are the similarities and differences between melting ionic compounds to conduct electricity and dissolving them?

♦ Andy ensures that every task has some kind of extension question or activity available for those who finish quickly. So that students know instantly where to find this task, he always highlights it in red on his slide-show. Over time, rather than asking 'What do I do next?', they get into the habit of 'looking for the red task'. Be wary though: you do not want students to embed bad habits because they rush to be the first to reach the extension!

♦ Give students a series of questions that move them incrementally from the factual to the inferential. For instance: What three items is the character wearing? What word does the writer use to describe his mood? Find two examples that demonstrate the character is feeling anxiety. What overall impression do you think the writer was attempting to create through these descriptions?

10. Direct Challenge

How do I account for the fact that students will need to be challenged at an individual level?

As we discussed at the start of this chapter, the most effective form of challenge is personalised and specific to individual students. The diagram below neatly sums up the interplay between the three factors that allows us to challenge our students.

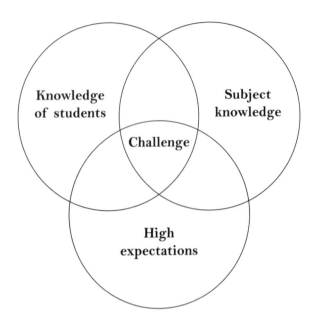

Your aim is to ensure that individuals are working at the optimal place – just outside their comfort zone. This is tougher than it sounds: for instance, Graham Nuthall's research suggests that, on average, 50% of what a child is learning about they already know.[9] Directed challenge is a simple but highly effective way of countering this problem, and it needs little preparation. It does, however, require a clear understanding from you about what the students need to know, or be able to do, next to progress. Once you are clear about this and the students are working on a task, simply move around the classroom and closely observe the work they are producing. Ask them specific questions that will move them on or provide them with the extra knowledge needed to approach the task in a more sophisticated way. The phrase 'Now try …' is especially useful.

For example, a student may be answering an extended question in geography on the impact of tourism on local communities. You notice that they have not supported their

---

9 Nuthall, *The Hidden Lives of Learners*, p. 35.

points with data. You then direct them to a table on employment figures in a textbook and say, 'Now try incorporating this new information into your answer.' You return later in the lesson to check that the improvement has been completed to a satisfactory standard. If it has you might say, 'Now try answering this question: what effect do you think unseasonable adverse weather conditions would have on these figures?'

While this is possibly one of the purest forms of differentiation, it is important to make it manageable.

♦ Focus on a set number of students each lesson. This is realistic and will ensure that, over time, all will receive this individual attention at a focused and in-depth level.

♦ Plan tasks that all students can be getting on with that will allow you to spend your time giving some students individual attention.

♦ To start with, plan some questions and 'Now try ...' examples that you can use. Over time, and as you grow more confident with the topic, you will probably not need to plan these in advance.

This strategy highlights how a complex teaching problem does not always require a complex solution.

11. Read for Breadth

How do we challenge students to pursue our subjects beyond the classroom?

Recently, an incredibly successful science teacher, Pam McCulloch, retired from our school. Her teaching laboratory had a huge selection of scientific journals and A level textbooks in it (bear in mind that Pam taught in a school without a sixth form). Her students were encouraged to read these books and journals to encourage a greater breadth to their knowledge. By immersing young people in scientific thought, Pam wanted to raise their expectations of what they could read, assimilate and enjoy both in and out of school. Eventually, such reading became the expectation in her classroom. It added a great richness and breadth to student knowledge, preparing them brilliantly for higher education.

However, we need to be realistic and accept that the reading ability of some students might preclude the effectiveness of this strategy. Nevertheless, our experiences in the classroom have shown us that, given the chance, young people never cease to confound expectations. Even though it might not be possible to fill every room with A level or degree-standard textbooks, modern technology allows us to implement this strategy with relative ease.

Here are a few ideas to consider:

- Introduce students to subject-specific websites such as BBC Science or National Geographic. Some teachers post QR codes around their classrooms and subject areas so students can access these quickly on their smartphones.

- Encourage your students to borrow subject-specific academic books from the library.

- Place books and reading material in students' hands yourself and ask them to regularly update you on their reading. The personal touch can go a long way.

- Send home subject-specific reading lists at the beginning of term for parents to purchase.

- Set up a subject-specific Twitter or Facebook account and use this to send students links to useful pages.

- Use the brilliant online tool https://padlet.com/ to post links to useful websites and encourage students to do likewise.

◆ Set up a class blog (there are many free blogging platforms to choose from, but WordPress is very easy to use and reliable). Students can then be given the responsibility of writing articles for the blog that relate to the topic being studied. The great thing about this is that it can be easily viewed and used by all students.

Extended reading is often regarded as the responsibility of English teachers. We feel, however, that more subjects could and should make this a priority. There is limited curriculum time available for teachers to develop the breadth of their students' knowledge, so all schools should be promoting wider reading, not just through fiction, but also through newspapers and other media.

12. Frame the Challenge

How do I embed a challenging classroom ethos through the language I use with students?

The language we use communicates our expectations of, and beliefs about, students' potential. Below are some phrases that we and other teachers have found successful. They take a bit of practice to get used to, but very soon they become second nature.

◆ Carol Dweck claims that 'yet' is one of the most powerful words we could use. So when a student says 'I can't do it,' we should end their sentence with 'yet!'

◆ 'If it's not excellent, it's not finished' is a great mantra for reinforcing the idea of continuous improvement and redrafting.

◆ Carol Dweck has coined the phrase, 'Working harder makes you smarter.'

- When a student is stuck, rather than giving them the answer straight away, use the response, 'Keep thinking about it. I'll come over in five minutes if you're still stuck.'

- 'There is no such thing as clever.' This is a useful phrase to open a discussion with students about growth and fixed mindsets. Rather than compounding the myth that intelligence is fixed and static, discuss the fact that intelligence can be developed by hard work and effort.

- If you believe that with extra time and thinking the student can realistically cope with the task, you could ask the question, 'What would you do if you weren't stuck?'

- When stuck, remind them of a time when they were not stuck and why they were not. This can sometimes spur them on to overcome the obstacle they are currently facing: 'I know you can do it because I remember ...'

- 'If you're not struggling, you're not learning.' We need to remind students that struggle is a good thing and not a sign of weakness.

- Education consultant Chris Moyse has developed a series of posters to be fixed to walls and doors that say, 'In this classroom we talk like ...' scientists, writers and so on.[10] The purpose is to encourage the use of subject-specific academic language.

---

10 Chris Moyse's blog is available at: http://chrismoyse.wordpress.com/.

Reflecting on Challenge

What matters most: the content itself or how I teach it?

The simple answer is both. A rich, challenging subject curriculum is a good starting point. This communicates high expectations to your students: whatever your academic starting point, whatever your socio-economic background, I aim to teach you knowledge and skills that matter in this world. If education is to be a great social equaliser, our students must leave us furnished with 'cultural capital' – the ideas and knowledge that can be drawn on to participate successfully in the intellectual, social and economic life of the land.

We are not arguing that schools should mindlessly reinforce the dominant power structures of society; rather that all young people are entitled to what educationalists Michael Young and David Lambert refer to as 'powerful knowledge'.[11] This is not 'fixed knowledge'; it is more flexible knowledge that should be open to critique, evolution and change. In simple terms, teach your English students *Great Expectations*, but be mindful that they do not take Dickens' slant on the world as gospel. Ask your students to critique the author's beliefs and attitudes to, say, women and religion.

Of course, a challenging curriculum must be offset by good teaching. Quite simply, hard content is harder to teach. Teaching *Great Expectations* to a class of Year 9s will require great finesse and patience. Students must be guided in careful steps, and ample time will need to be forged from a saturated curriculum. Breadth will have to be sacrificed for depth. You, as the teacher, will struggle too.

---

11 Michael Young and David Lambert, *Knowledge and the Future School: Curriculum and Social Justice* (London: Bloomsbury Academic, 2014).

Our day-to-day classroom experiences have repeatedly shown us that students appreciate being told, 'This is hard, but in time I believe you can get there.' That is why this chapter on challenge comes first in this book, and why we believe it sets in motion all that follows.

Must every lesson be challenging?

No. This would be a mistake. Perhaps the most crucial strategy in this chapter is The Long Haul. As we have discussed, challenge is about taking students on a long journey via small, solid steps. Sometimes you will have to go backwards to go forwards. This is where challenge can become easily misunderstood. New learning needs to be presented in a coherent order that builds on the previous topic. If a child is not secure in a concept, and they are moved on too swiftly, they will carry their knowledge gaps and misconceptions through to the next topic. Over time they will form habits that are increasingly difficult to budge and gaps that are difficult to fill.

One of the criticisms made of the now-discarded national curriculum levels is that they encouraged teachers to move students on too quickly.[12] Rather than being given the chance to extend and master understanding of a topic – say, long division in maths – students were swiftly moved on to a more difficult topic before they were secure in the first area. This would then take on the guise of 'progress' up the artificial numerical grading system, even if the topic needed to be re-taught in its entirety next year because it had not been fully mastered in the first place.

Our simple suggestion is this: if students clearly do not know, or cannot do, something – even if by their age and key

---

12 See Tim Oates, Assessment Without Levels in Depth [video] (n.d.). Available at: http://www.cambridgeassessment.org.uk/insights/assessment-without-levels-extended-version-tim-oates-insights/.

stage they really should – then teach it until they do, whether your teaching would seem to meet the 'official' definition of challenging or not.

Be careful that you do not conflate challenge with 'task difficulty', which are two different things. Let's say your English class need to learn the meaning of two challenging terms, 'poignancy' and 'ambiguity'. You might be tempted to make this task more difficult by asking them to search for definitions in the dictionary. However, this makes learning the words harder, not easier. The child has to (a) find the word, (b) comprehend its meaning and (c) consider how this meaning might apply to a range of written and real-world scenarios. A more efficient use of your time would be to teach the students the meaning of the two words, and then focus your attention on giving them relevant examples and time to practise the words correctly in a range of contexts.

The take-away is this: always look for the easiest path to learning challenging material, not the hardest.

How do I motivate my students to accept tough challenges?

When we hear and read entreaties that we 'challenge students' as much as we possibly can, we tend to nod in agreement. It seems a no-brainer for the first few seconds … Then the insidious thoughts creep in. Vivid and uninvited images of our most inert and recalcitrant students slumped and dribbling over their desks reveal themselves in all their glory. We wonder, 'How am I going to motivate this lot to embrace the challenge? Keeping them engaged is a challenge in itself!' And so the doubts set in.

There are two counters to this. First, on the psychological front, we need to replace the 'dribbling Joe' images with those of our keenest, most focused students – who usually make up the majority. Can we deny the majority in favour of the minority? Should we be making excuses for our subjects by teaching inferior material in the hope that children will enjoy it more?

Second, it is worth reflecting on the findings from educational research. The Sutton Trust's *What Makes Great Teaching?* report is clear that the best way to motivate students is *through* the content we teach them. Attempts to motivate students *before* we teach them content tend to be unsuccessful. Motivation usually comes from understanding, not before it. The report also highlights that great teaching constantly asks for more from students, yet does not forget about the importance of their self-worth.[13]

Which teaching strategies will allow challenge to come to life in my classroom?

This is the focus of the rest of this book. Once a challenging ethos has been set, it is time to match it with great teaching. The starting point lies in how we explain new and difficult material in a way that students will both understand and remember.

---

13 Coe et al., *What Makes Great Teaching?*, p. 23.

Chapter 2
Explanation

Year 7 Geography with John

John wants his mixed-ability Year 7 students to love geography. He wants them to discover the subject as if it were a treasure chest buried on a deserted island. His latest topic, 'Climate in the Subtropics', could easily become as dry as the deserts themselves, so John sets up his lesson as a series of workstations. A case study from a different subtropical region of the globe is placed at each desk. Apart from the rules of the task, John explains nothing. Students are to synthesise information from the case studies as they circulate around the workstations in small groups. The learning objective is 'single and challenging': by the end of the lesson he wants students to be able to identify and explain the key features of subtropical climates.

As the lesson draws to a close, John asks his students what they have learnt. Most understand that the subtropics are characterised by high average temperatures and low rainfall. When he asks for further identification of the main features, many students fixate on small details: 'In the Sahara Desert temperatures can reach over 50 degrees Celsius' and 'There is little wind in subtropical Argentina.' Many struggle to distinguish the unifying features that characterise all subtropical regions from the divergent details of the individual case studies. Few Year 7s can piece everything together to form a clear understanding. They have enjoyed the lesson – but how many have learnt anything at a deep level?

Declan

Declan is an academically able Year 10 student. He loves maths and science and hopes one day to study medicine at university. He is excited to discover that his new physics teacher, Mr Brennan, is a graduate in astrophysics. The subject is Mr Brennan's life's passion – so much so that he has eschewed the lure of academia to share his love of physics with the next generation.

Unfortunately, though, Mr Brennan struggles to communicate his knowledge to his students. Even Declan – so keen – cannot make head nor tail of Mr Brennan's lengthy and well-meaning explanations. In Mr Brennan's mind, he explains new concepts simply and clearly; in Declan's mind, these same words and sentences are an impossibly complex jumble of technical terminology.

Explanation –
What It Is and Why It Matters

In the past decade or so, teacher explanation seems to have become unfashionable in the UK and, in some quarters, frowned upon. Some in the profession argue that teacher talk is dull and didactic, actively preventing children from constructing meaning independently. They suggest that talk should be kept to a minimum, with the teacher taking on the role of facilitator – as in John's Year 7 geography lessons. We believe, however, that high quality teacher talk is the first step in creating a classroom ethos of excellence and growth.

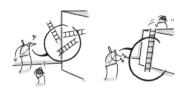

Admittedly, some teachers – like Declan's Mr Brennan – know much about their subject but struggle to make it comprehensible for students. Even so, just because some teacher talk can miss its target or over-dominate lessons, it does not follow that all extended teacher talk should be tarnished with the same brush. Indeed, in your best explanations, your artistry with words will transform complicated and abstract material into something clear and meaningful. Explanation is one of the master arts of the classroom. This chapter, therefore, will argue that the humble explanation should be brought back to its rightful place at the heart of good practice. We will then suggest a number of time-honoured and evidence-supported techniques to help you to improve the quality of your explanations.

There is an ever-growing body of evidence to support the claim that teacher-led instruction is more effective than asking students to discover new knowledge and skills for themselves. In 2006, Kirschner, Sweller and Clark concluded that minimal guidance – when teachers like Mr Brown take a back seat and act mainly as facilitators – had been consistently shown by empirical studies to be less effective than teacher-led instruction.[1] Likewise, educationalist John Hattie,

---

1 Paul A. Kirschner, John Sweller and Richard E. Clark, Why Minimal Guidance During Instruction Does Not Work: An Analysis of the Failure of Constructivist, Discovery, Problem-Based, Experiential, and Inquiry-Based Teaching, *Educational Psychologist* 41(2) (2006): 75–86.

who has synthesised 800 meta-analyses, has reported that direct teacher instruction and instructional quality have two of the top three effect sizes. In other words, along with feedback, classroom strategies that give teacher explanation a central role have more impact on learning than many others.[2]

There are three principles that define the best explanations. The first is that they should be tethered to something students already know about. For example, to explain to a child how to use an adverbial phrase you should start by reactivating their knowledge of the adverb. To explain to a child how to divide with decimals you should start by asking them to recall the procedure used to divide whole numbers. To explain to a child the structure of the feudal system you should begin by alluding to the way modern society is organised. The fact is that we learn in the context of what we already know.[3] As we have seen, one of Mr Brennan's shortcomings was that he did not take into account that Declan's and his own prior knowledge did not match.

The second is that explanations should allow for the limited capacity of the human memory to hold on to a number of new ideas at once. As such, new ideas should be introduced in short, manageable increments. This is why the students in John's Year 7 geography lesson, described above, struggled to grasp the unifying features of subtropical climates. They had been given too much to think about in one go. If John had explained the key features clearly and concisely, one by one, *before* setting the class to work on the case studies, students' working memories would have been less compromised.

The final ingredient of the successful explanation is that it should aim to transform abstract ideas into concrete ones. The best teachers are skilled at making complex ideas seem clear and simple without losing any of the inherent

2   John Hattie, *Visible Learning: A Synthesis of Over 800 Meta-Analyses Relating to Achievement* (New York: Routledge, 2009).
3   Willingham, *Why Don't Students Like School?*, p. 88.

complexity. It's no easy feat. Maths teachers have to explain calculus, science teachers have to bring atomic particles to life, English teachers have to point out the subtleties of irony. The clarity and concision of your language use is vital in helping students to understand and remember these difficult concepts.

So, high quality explanation *is* important. The best teacher explanations, however, are defined not by the theatricality of their delivery but by the subtlety of their design. Not only do they involve a passing of knowledge from one mind to another (not that it happens that simply!) but they are also delivered in a way that will assist in the student's long-term recall of the material.

Much of this chapter is inspired by Chip and Dan Heath's wonderful book, *Made to Stick*.[4] After scrutinising many ideas – from fields as diverse as low-cost airline marketing to Bill Clinton's US election campaign slogan – they have sketched out a blueprint for 'stickability'. Ideas that stick are those that will leave a lasting impression in the listener's memory so that they are hard to forget. Excitingly, the recipe they suggest can be used and manipulated by anyone who has an important message to communicate. It is gold dust for the classroom teacher. Their six 'sticky' principles are easy to remember by the mnemonic SUCCES: simple, unexpected, concrete, credible, emotional and story.

How can we make our teaching 'stick'?

Sticking trait	Explanation
Simple	Choose the core concepts that need to be understood and communicate these – anchor them to what students already know.

---

4   Chip Heath and Dan Heath, *Made to Stick: Why Some Ideas Take Hold and Others Come Unstuck* (London: Arrow Books, 2007).

Unexpected	Generate curiosity by highlighting and opening up gaps in their knowledge.
Concrete	Provide the opportunities for students to do something that makes the concept real and meaningful.
Credible	Provide the opportunities for students to see or experience something that will make them believe the concept.
Emotional	Make students 'feel' something as a result of your teaching e.g. empathy, sympathy, aspiration.
Story	Tell a story around the concept – especially if it has a human/ personal element to it.

A good explanation need not include every one of these features, but it would certainly contain a flavour of them. Many of the strategies we share in this chapter draw from the Heath brothers' suggestions.

Central to any explanation must be a teacher's subject knowledge. Only with secure and confident knowledge can we be artful with our talk; indeed, we would argue that a student's progress is partly bound to the depth and breadth of her teacher's subject knowledge (remember Know Thy Subject from Chapter 1).

Be that as it may, there is a danger lurking in the shadows. The Heath brothers characterise it as 'the curse of knowledge'. As subject experts who are comfortably fluent in our own knowledge, it is easy to forget what it is like to be a novice. We have already seen how Declan's teacher, Mr Brennan, is hindered by an empathy gap – an inability to envision the prior knowledge of a child and the stages that he or she will need to go through to reach understanding – when trying to explain complex physics to secondary school children.

Try imagining that you do not know a piece of information that you now take for granted – for instance, that 9 x 9 is 81, or that the word 'pneumonia' begins with a 'p', or that the Battle of Hastings occurred in 1066. It is really hard to imagine that another person might not know these facts or find it difficult to learn them when they come so easily to you. Your knowledge is effortlessly recalled. But, unfortunately, your students do not have access to your mind and its rich store of knowledge built up over a lifetime.

Now for a more extreme example. Take this description of water potential, a topic covered in biology:

The potential energy of the water molecules is called the water potential. Water will diffuse from a region of high water potential to a region of lower water potential, and the steeper the water potential gradient the greater will be the tendency for water to diffuse in this direction. For practical purposes we can therefore define water potential as the capacity of a system to lose water.

Consider the vocabulary expectations here: *diffuse, molecules, region* and *gradient*. The writer has made plenty of assumptions: we already know and understand this technical vocabulary, we are well-acquainted with key biological concepts and we have the necessary faculties to synthesise such dense information. An experienced scientist will almost certainly comprehend such written explanations with ease. For the rest of us, however, the density of the language creates a barrier to understanding. We need a teacher to unpick it with us.

Explanation is possibly the hardest pedagogical principle in this book to master. To an extent, you need to unlearn your expert knowledge so that you can reformulate it into a teachable material. To use a more concrete image – quite literally! – you should begin by constructing the tower block of your expertise, bulldoze it down and carefully rebuild it. This time, in the words, phrases, imagery and incremental steps – the bricks, mortar and girders – that will have meaning for the apprentice builders in your charge. This is often known as *pedagogical content knowledge*, which is defined by a teacher's understanding of how to adapt teaching approaches to fit the specific needs of the subject content.

Teachers are so often encouraged to talk less. While this can sometimes be helpful advice – some teacher talk is overlong and lacks focus – surely a better idea is to work on how to talk better. Explanation is an exciting and often underexplored skill which lies at the heart of good classroom practice. Your explanation should be carefully planned, yet it will also need to be improvised in response to the ever-evolving needs of your students. Explanations go hand in hand with modelling, are enhanced by regular and targeted questioning, introduce content for students to practise and are informed by the feedback we receive back from students.

In truth, explanations are the bedrock on which all future learning is built.

1. Find the Sweet Spot

What is the optimal starting point for my explanation?

It is usually best to begin by activating your class's prior knowledge. This serves a double function: first, it means that your explanation is less likely to repeat what they already know and, second, it helps students to form concrete links between new content and their existing knowledge – a process fundamental to learning.

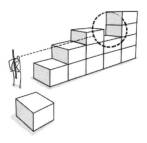

At the start of any scheme of learning, lesson or increase in difficulty, it is vital to identify the sweet spot between what they know/can do and what they do not know/cannot do before unleashing your explanation. Recently, Andy opened a sequence of Year 9 English lessons on Arthur Conan Doyle's Sherlock Holmes story, 'The Adventure of the Speckled Band', by asking his students to write down and explain what they already knew about Holmes. The recent TV series meant that many had some understanding already. They knew, for instance, that Holmes is a detective with a sidekick called Watson, who displays strange personal characteristics. Yet this knowledge was patchy and littered with obvious misconceptions – such as the curious notion that Sherlock Holmes was a historical figure who existed in real life!

This initial task allowed Andy to find the sweet spot so that he could build his explanations on the class's prior knowledge. In the explanation and the class discussion that ensued, he took the opportunity to take up and extend the strands the class had introduced themselves. He taught them, among other things, the meaning of the word 'idiosyncratic' to describe Holmes and clarified why Holmes' reliance on deduction and logical reasoning would have appealed to Conan Doyle's science and technology obsessed Victorian readership.

Barak Rosenshine, who brought together research on master teachers, cognitive science and cognitive supports, has highlighted that activating prior knowledge is a fundamental trait of good teaching.[5] There are plenty of simple strategies that you can use in every lesson to do this:

♦ Start with a short quiz that looks back to the previous lesson and even further back. It need be only a few questions in length – perhaps only one. As students feed-back the answers, it allows you to both go over anything they have forgotten or misunderstood from last lesson and to take up and develop the strands that will lead them into the new lesson or topic. (We explore this strategy in more depth in Build Memory Platforms in Chapter 4.)

♦ Ask students to formulate their own questions on the areas they are struggling with or do not understand. They can narrow these down to one question in pairs or perhaps fours. Once the questions are decided on, you can then dedicate a few minutes to answering them in front of the whole class.

♦ Nominate one or two designated 'questioners' in every group. This role works most effectively if it is given to a confident student who is not afraid to voice their confusion or uncertainty. More often than not, they will express the concerns of the majority and so provide you with the perfect sweet spot to spur your explanation.

♦ Lee Ridout, a very successful maths teacher at our school, starts his lessons with one task on the board. For example:

Remember we struggled with _____ *last lesson. Do you remember why we didn't like answering equations like the one below?*

---

5 Barak Rosenshine, Principles of Instruction: Research-Based Strategies That All Teachers Should Know, *American Educator* 36(1) (2012): 12–19. Available at: https://www.aft.org/sites/default/files/periodicals/Rosenshine.pdf.

The beauty of this strategy is that it enables Lee to pin-point exactly where and how his students are struggling, so that he can take his lesson on from this point. (Note, too, the deliberate use of 'we' rather than 'you'. Lee seeks to empathise with the students in their struggles so that learning in his maths lessons becomes a joint, collegiate mission.)

2. Know Thy Misconceptions

Aside from knowing my subject inside out, how else can I prepare my explanations?

In the last chapter we shared the fundamental Know Thy Subject strategy. Yet knowing your subject well is not enough in itself. You also need to know the common pitfalls, errors and misunderstandings associated with the topic. Unlike Declan's physics teacher, you must try to think like a student. The best teachers are skilled empathisers. This takes time to learn.

Over time, you will come to know the main misconceptions in your subject area – the traps students regularly fall into and the obstacles that present themselves along the way. For instance, Andy has learnt that when teaching the possessive apostrophe, many students fall into the trap of indiscriminately using an apostrophe in any word ending with 's'. So, 'Shaun walks to work' becomes 'Shaun walk's to work'. Teaching the new concept solves a problem and creates a new one simultaneously. This problem is true to many topics students encounter at school.

This is why knowing and understanding the common misconceptions encountered by students studying your subject is so important. Andy, by employing some of the strategies we explain below, has learnt that he needs to spend time seeing off this misunderstanding further upstream in the teaching cycle.

Here are some strategies that we and others at our school find effective:

Lead Students Into The Trap

Design your teaching episodes so that students are drawn into making obvious mistakes. When teaching John Steinbeck's *Of Mice and Men*, Andy allows students to make simplistic assumptions about the character of Curley's wife: 'She's a flirt', 'She's vain and self-centred' or 'All she is after is one thing!' Then, through deeper questioning and explanation, he guides students into an understanding that Curley's wife's obvious behaviour is a front, a facade behind which lies a vulnerable, lonely and misunderstood girl, a victim of a misogynist world. By leading students into this set-up, and then lifting them out again, they may be less likely to succumb to simplistic interpretations of the next character they meet in the novel. If a student has held a misconception before and now understands how they were mistaken, they are unlikely to fall in the same trap again.

Do the Work Yourself

Spend less time planning bells-and-whistles slide-shows and more time having a go at the work your students will complete yourself before the lesson. A history teacher might write the essay she expects students to complete before teaching the sequence that leads up to it, a maths teacher might complete a complex equation or an English teacher might annotate a poem. If you have done it yourself, you are more likely to predict and pre-empt the pitfalls students will face. You will have a better understanding of the aspects that require careful modelling and explanation.

Keep a Record of Common Misconceptions

A useful task is to start writing down common misconceptions that you encounter in each topic, so that next time you teach it you can return to these and incorporate them into your teaching before they create problems for the class. The maths and science departments in our school are now mapping out and recording common misconceptions – and the best ways to help students to avoid them – across their respective curriculums. An advantage of creating an inventory like this is that it can be shared with new, inexperienced teachers to prevent them from making the same mistakes as their colleagues.

Tell Stories

As you are explaining a new topic, narrate stories of previous students and classes, and the avoidable mistakes they have made. We provide an example in the Become a Storyteller strategy on page 69.

3. Explain First

Should I prepare my explanations in advance, or hope that students will give me the correct answer in response to my questioning?

Unsurprisingly, students will often have little prior knowledge of the concept they are about to learn about. Take this classroom exchange for instance:

You: Who knows the definition of oxymoron?

Ryan: Is it, like, a really silly cow?

Megan: Is it a contrast between two things?

You: Getting closer …

Fred: I know. It's a really small cow – like a contrast?

This discussion could drag on for ages with everybody, you included, becoming more and more confused. In fact, involving the class here has backfired and created a number of avoidable misconceptions. Indeed, even after you have put the class straight, Fred still might leave the lesson genuinely believing that an oxymoron really is a small cow – children do tend to remember their oral contribution to lessons!

Now here is an example of a teacher who has thought about and prepared her explanation in advance:

An oxymoron occurs when we place two opposite terms next to each other. It's a part of everyday life. Put your hand up if you have ever felt 'sweet sorrow' – happy and sad at the same time. Yes, me too. Only this morning I felt 'sweet sorrow'. I was sad to say goodbye to my son, but happy to see that he was waving at me through the window with a huge smile on his face. Another good example of an oxymoron is 'deafening

silence' or 'alone together'. Both phrases contain words with
opposite meanings next to each other, as do all oxymorons.
Who can think of any more oxymorons?

In this example, the teacher uses several examples supported
by a real-life anecdote – which pulls on the heartstrings just
a little – before attempting to involve the students. When
you foresee that students will be completely new to a topic
or fact, it is simply more efficient and effective to begin with
the explanation and involve the students later. This is especially true when introducing new vocabulary.

Ascertaining what the students already know and involving
them in your explanation are important strategies. But every
time the phrase 'Who knows?' comes to your lips, think carefully about whether you need to use it, especially if you have
a suspicion that this idea is unlikely to have been encountered before.

Be very mindful about referring students to the dictionary
too. To correctly interpret a dictionary definition of an unfamiliar word, reading ability and general knowledge will
need to be strong. Here's the Oxford English Dictionary's
description of 'oxymoron' for you:

n. a figure of speech or expressed idea in which apparently
contradictory terms appear in conjunction: 'affordable caviar'
need not be an oxymoron.

This definition would make understanding what an oxymoron is even harder for most children. The child has to know
what 'caviar' is first, along with how 'conjunction' applies to
this context. Once again, the carefully crafted teacher explanation – tailored to the needs and understanding of the class
– is by far the better option.

Should we, therefore, avoid difficult vocabulary in our explanations? Of course not. We just need to be heedful that we

do not overcomplicate things. When you use or read new vocabulary with your class, try slipping in an aside to explain the meaning of the word without interrupting your flow – for example: 'The novel exposes the marginalisation – that means being pushed to one side and forgotten about by the rest of the world – of women and the elderly.'

4. Open the Gap

How can I use explanation to tap into a child's natural sense of curiosity?

Intriguingly, researchers have found that generation – struggling to find answers to problems before receiving guidance from a teacher – can aid long-term memory retention.[6] Although this may seem to contradict the previous strategy, it does not. Note that we are not relying on students to provide the solution. We will fill in the knowledge gaps, but a little later after they have had a go on their own. Nor should this be confused with the example of John's Year 7 geography class at the start of this chapter who were given little to no guidance before they began the carousel task.

The Heath brothers introduced us to the work of behavioural economist George Loewenstein, who in 1994 developed gap theory: 'Loewenstein argues that gaps cause pain. When we want to know something but don't, it's like having an itch we need to scratch. To take away the pain, we need to fill the knowledge gap.'[7] The trick, then, is to sometimes deliberately withhold knowledge for a short while to spark curiosity.

---

6   Peter C. Brown, Henry L. Roediger III and Mark A. McDaniel, *Make It Stick: The Science of Successful Learning* (Cambridge, MA: Harvard University Press, 2014), p. 87.

7   Heath and Heath, *Made to Stick*, p. 84.

You might want to try some of the following strategies:

♦ Ask students to make predictions and estimations at the start of the lesson by utilising the knowledge they already have on a topic. For example: which character is most likely to reveal a terrible secret in the story today? What would happen if the Bank of England went bankrupt? If a hammer and feather were dropped from the same height on the moon, which would reach the ground first?

♦ Construct your lesson or explanation as a story or mystery. For instance, rather than beginning your geography lesson on tsunamis with, 'Today we are going to learn about tsunamis,' start by narrating a tale from the point of view of a tsunami victim. Narrate the story, dropping in key geographical details as you go. You might begin with a description of an ordinary day, before moving on to a vivid account of the earthquake itself, followed by the panic and confusion of the tidal wave, finishing with a report of the human and structural devastation in the aftermath. This will give the subject the human and emotional impact that a statement like 'Over 2,000 people were killed and over 50,000 displaced' does not. The facts, figures and geographical concepts can then be built on to this emotive 'hook' later.

♦ Create mystery out of ordinary topics. For example, when introducing ratio and proportion in maths, show students a copy of Da Vinci's 'Vitruvian Man' sketch and get them to come up with possible proportions in the human body that they will then go on to work out using mathematical procedures.

5. Keep the Main Thing the Main Thing

How do I use clear, simple language and avoid waffling?

In his book for new English teachers, Alex Quigley writes that a good explanation should 'have the power of compressed language'. He writes also of the importance of speaking in 'patterns' of subject-specific language.[8] He is dead right. Concision and repetition are central to the great explanation.

If the focus for your maths lesson is rounding decimals, then be sure to keep returning to your key terminology (e.g. rounding, decimal, place value) frequently as the lesson progresses. A core message should be both simple and repeated regularly.

When introducing new content it is wise to keep your sentences grammatically short and simple. Students can lose track if your sentences are open and begin with subordinate clauses like the following:

Although the …

Contrary to popular opinion …

Taking that into account …

Instead, frontload your sentences with the key learning point:

---

8   Alex Quigley, *Teach Now! English: Becoming a Great English Teacher* [Kindle edn] (Abingdon: Routledge, 2014), loc. 1943.

Calculate the circumference of a circle by …

A metaphor is …

Volley the ball with …

However, once students become secure in these concepts, it is important to model and promote more complex academic language as you move from surface to deep learning, guiding the class towards linking together and synthesising these ideas. Consider explanations as a sliding scale: start them concise and concrete, and build up the complexity as you go. (We explore modelling academic speech and thought further in Show Them How to Speak in Chapter 3.)

6. Become a Storyteller

How can I increase the chances that children will remember what I tell them?

Psychologists have discovered that stories are 'psychologically privileged' in the human mind.[9] As a species, we seem to be primed to remember narrative in more depth than most other forms of information input. As teachers, it is important that we harness this effect to the full. Stories are wonderfully efficient resources: we transport them in our minds. They require no photocopying, PowerPoint slides or glue sticks.

We have found that as soon as we begin to tell a story, a remarkable transformation comes about in the room. Pens are put down, eyes focus on our lips and any fidgeting is

---

9   Willingham, *Why Don't Students Like School?*, p. 66.

replaced by a Zen-like stillness. There is a profound and mysterious magic to stories.

There are countless ways to use storytelling in your lessons, but here are three we have found to be particularly effective.

Tell Stories About Your Past Students

All of us remember fondly those past students whose attributes we would like our current classes to emulate. It might have been their capacity for effort, the way they took criticism on the chin or the way they never gave up in the face of setbacks. This example comes from history teacher and blogger Harry Fletcher-Wood, and is about Holly, a student who modelled the importance of asking questions:

Holly questioned everything. She wouldn't let an idea go, just kept asking and asking and asking, until she was satisfied she understood. This process took time, but everyone benefitted, because she made certain that things made sense to her before she let me, or the class, move on (when you're unravelling the US constitution this can take a while). Her determination to learn meant she always did, so she was wildly successful.

Holly made planning easy: all I had to do was present a stimulus or a problem and let her get her teeth into it. This determination could make me lazy: I could guarantee an excellent discussion which would push me and the class. Holly illustrates the power of asking questions and taking responsibility for, and insisting on, understanding.

Tell Personal Anecdotes

Some students find it difficult to believe that teachers are living, breathing human beings with personal lives beyond the classroom. Anecdotes from teachers' personal lives fascinate them, especially if these titbits of information are drip-fed over time. Quite often, a child Shaun taught years before will stop him in the corridor to ask him about Subbuteo – Shaun once won a local championship and uses his story to exemplify the importance of regular deliberate practice (see Chapter 4).

Andy also uses a personal story when teaching First World War poetry to his GCSE students:

When I first moved into my new house, a Victorian terraced cottage built in the 1880s, my partner wanted to find out about its previous residents. Who had walked up and down the same stairway a century before? Who had once slept in the same room that we sleep in every night? Who had lived and died under this roof? One Saturday morning, she googled our address only to find that it came up on a public records website. Living in our house in 1918 had been a family of three just like us: a mother, a father and their son. The tragic part came next. She then found our address on another website, a site that listed the names of those who died in action during the First World War. The boy's name was on the list. Killed on the Somme in 1918.

Andy uses this story to help emphasise the cruel sadness of war poems such as Wilfred Owen's 'Futility'. Students can sometimes struggle to grasp the emotional impact of such poems; death can seem unreal, like an event from fiction. This story helps Andy to illustrate that the 'limbs, so dear-achieved', written about so powerfully by Owen, were those of ordinary young people, living in ordinary homes with ordinary families, like their own.

Turn Misconceptions Into Stories

A useful approach is to tell stories of the common misconceptions made by previous classes in the hope that the next cohort will sidestep the same hazards. When explaining how to use a thesaurus effectively, Andy shares the following story:

A Year 9 boy I once taught was desperate to improve the range of vocabulary he used in his writing. He had written down the sentence, 'He walked slowly into the room.' He wanted to use a more evocative adverb than 'slowly' so he looked the word up in the thesaurus. There was no entry for 'slowly' but there was for 'slow'. He skimmed down the list until his eye fell on the word 'retard'. Ah, he thought. If I turn retard into an adverb then I will be crafting a more subtle sentence. The sentence he wrote was, 'He walked retardedly into the room.' He had quite unwittingly written something that could be regarded as offensive.

Andy uses this anecdote to guide students towards understanding why they should use thesauruses cautiously. Synonyms do not just replace one another like for like – they are differentiated by shades of meaning. The teaching point is clear: it is wise to use a thesaurus to find words you already understand rather than as a means of shoehorning totally new words into your sentences.

There are many rich and varied ways that stories can be used to enrich learning – those above are the tip of the iceberg. Local interest stories, national news reports and fascinating tales from the rich history of your subject all provide ripe pickings in a range of learning contexts.

7. Tap Into the Power of Analogy

How can I make complex, abstract ideas simpler to understand?

Analogy is the bread and butter of teacher explanation. By comparing a new concept to an idea already securely fastened in your listeners' knowledge, there is a good chance they will comprehend it quickly.

Inference is the bedfellow of analogy. If you described, for example, the human long-term memory as the brain's internal hard-drive, your listener should infer that this is the place in the mind where secure memories are saved. For an analogy to work, such links must be made. If, however, your listener has no knowledge of the inner workings of a computer then your analogy will not only fail, but will also confound understanding even more. Once again, having a strong understanding of students' prior knowledge is crucial.

A successful analogy will take the class on a journey from the concrete to the abstract. For instance, to demonstrate that a hydrogen atom contains one proton in the nucleus and is surrounded by one electron, science teachers will ask students to imagine a grain of rice in a sports stadium. If the grain – the proton – is placed in the middle of the pitch, the outer row of seats are the limit of the electron's influence, while the remainder of the atom is empty space. Like the rest of the seats, the electron seems to be everywhere at once.[10]

This analogy works because almost all students know what a grain of rice looks like and will have some grasp of the

---

10 Example adapted from Allan G. Harrison and Richard K. Coll (eds), *Using Analogies in Middle and Secondary Science Classrooms: The FAR Guide – An Interesting Way to Teach with Analogies* (Thousand Oaks, CA: Corwin, 2008), pp. 133–134.

dimensions of a large sports arena. However, there is a snag. Analogies do not always give the full picture. There are often fundamental differences between the analogy and the target idea. In this case, a two-dimensional analogy (the sports stadium) has been used to explain a three-dimensional phenomenon (the atom).

The solution is to introduce the analogy to allow students to construct the rough idea, but then use further explanation to dismantle the analogy and identify its differences from the target knowledge. In this case, the differences between a stadium and the inner workings of an atom.

The following table gives an idea of how you might plan your use of analogies.

Like misconceptions and stories, the best analogies should be shared widely. They are vital teaching tools.

8. Give Multiple Examples

What if my first explanation is unsuccessful?

Bearing in mind that every student you teach brings slightly different prior knowledge to the table, one explanation on its own is often not enough. The more examples and strategies we have up our sleeves in readiness, the better.

Our colleague, Lee Ridout, takes an interesting approach. If a student does not understand his initial explanation, he places the blame on himself rather than the student. If at first he does not succeed, he will try a different tact and, if that is also unsuccessful, he will try another approach and another. Lee is tenacious. He never views the child as incapable of learning. He always believes that there is a way – he just has to find it.

The target idea	What is the key idea that you want to get across?	The structure of the atom.
The analogy	What analogy will you use to explain this idea?	A grain of rice in the middle of the pitch in an empty stadium and a speck of dust on a seat on the outermost row of seats.
The similarities	What are the similarities between the analogy and real life?	The grain of rice is the proton in the nucleus of the atom. The speck of dust is the electron. The whole stadium is the hydrogen atom.
The sticking points	What are some of the key points that you want the analogy to get across to the students?	Electrons have very little mass compared to protons. Electrons are on the outside of the atom. Between the nucleus and the electrons is mostly empty space.
Take away the differences	What are the differences between the analogy and real life? How will this help students to find real meaning?	Atoms are 3D objects. The electron is not static (like the speck of dust) – it orbits the nucleus. The space between the grain of rice and the speck of dust still contains matter (grass, seats, etc.). In an atom, the space between the nucleus and electrons is empty (i.e. it is a vacuum).

Let's take a geography lesson on glacier formation. A skilled and prepared teacher might have the following examples and explanation strategies ready to use as required:

♦ A concise description linked to prior knowledge – a slow-moving river of ice.

♦ A physical re-enactment in the form of a slow-moving line of students at the front of the class. The teacher adds a new student every now and again at one end to represent the zone of accumulation (where the snow falls) and takes away one at the other end to represent the zone of ablation (where the glacier melts away).

♦ A range of visual images and diagrams to point out the key knowledge.

♦ A series of questions that will target common misconceptions.

If none of these are successful, like Lee, the teacher will need to go back to the drawing board. The best explainers never give up.

9. Bring the Room to Life

Help, I need to improvise an explanation – where do I start?

The easiest place to start is by making an associative link with your immediate environment. Indeed, there is something quite magical about transforming a student's perception of their surroundings through language alone. The strategies below work well for both planned and improvised explanations.

Features of the Physical Environment

Help the students to visualise ideas by making analogies with the physical world of the classroom. 'Look at the tiny square windows on the wall up there, behind you. The only light the men would receive would be through windows just like those,' is one way Andy has helped his students to grasp the atmosphere John Steinbeck portrays in his claustrophobic description of the bunkhouse in *Of Mice and Men.*

Similarly, maths teachers, when explaining how to calculate volume, might reinforce their message by demonstrating how to measure the volume of the classroom itself in cubic metres before moving on to more abstract examples. A history teacher might be lucky enough to be in the position to ask her students to look out of the window at a Norman church spire in the distance: 'That very church was built by the invaders from France who used their architecture to assert their authority and might.'

Link People to Concepts

Statistics, numbers and percentages tend to be quite abstract representations of concrete truths. One way to tackle this is to get into the habit of using students as physical representations. To demonstrate that 10–15% of slaves died during the Middle Passage, a history teacher could ask three to five members of the class to stand: 'If we, as a class, were a group of slaves on the slave boats, those who are sitting would have survived.' This makes the cruel human impact of slavery much more real to the class than the numbers themselves, which can be difficult to comprehend on their own and can obscure the personal suffering of the victims.

To teach the difference between fate and free will, Andy hands out playing cards arbitrarily to half the class members which they place face down on their tables. The other half of the class are given nothing. As those students with cards reveal them, Andy reads from a list of pre-prepared notes. For example: 'The ace of spades. You're lucky – you'll live to the ripe old age of one-hundred' or 'The three of hearts. Not so lucky. You will die alone and unhappy.' Those who have been given cards have had their futures decided for them – the card represents their inevitable fate. Those without cards, on the other hand, can shape their futures as they wish. They have free will.

Tableaux and Physical Re-enactments

Using students as physical representations of ideas is a classic strategy – and rather fun too. English teachers will often ask a handful of students up to the front to bring to life a scene from a text. The rest of the class help position the volunteers by making close references to textual evidence. The teacher can then question the class on the playwright's use of stage directions and move students (characters) as necessary. Some science teachers take a whole class outside onto the playing field to recreate a human model of the solar system. If you want students to understand just how far away Pluto is, they will never forget the speck that is little Johnny, cold and alone, slouching disconsolately in the staff car park!

Hypothetical Scenarios

If the classroom itself does not quite cut the associative mustard then it is time to bring in the imagination. When teaching the poem 'Mametz Wood' by Owen Sheers – which features the unearthing of skeletons of forgotten First World War soldiers – to emphasise the physical proximity of history, Andy asks his students to imagine what secrets of the past might be lurking unheard a mere couple of metres under the classroom carpet ...

If you are teaching a class about the ethical theory of utilitarianism – the idea that actions are morally right if they benefit the majority – then ask the students to imagine that a man has just entered the room with a gun. A utilitarian stance would suggest that you, the teacher, should hit him over the head with your metre ruler to protect the class. One death will save the lives of many.

10. Involve Them

Should my students sit quietly as I talk at them?

The notion that students do not learn well through passive listening is a myth, pure and simple. They can and do learn in this way.[11] Nevertheless, they must be listening and paying attention. To ensure this, our explanations should be interactive. So far we have covered a few strategies that allow this to happen such as Open the Gap and Bring the Room to Life. Here are a few more.

Communicate with Your Body Language

In his classic 1970s book on successful classroom management, *The Craft of the Classroom*, former head teacher Michael Marland recommended the following:

The key is communication with your eyes. Feel the sectors of the room, and underline the structure and sequence of your

11 See Coe et al., *What Makes Great Teaching?*, p. 24.

remarks by directing phrases to the different sectors ... Within each group, look only at one pupil, a different one each time you return to the sector, and cast your remark to him.[12]

Where you position yourself, how you position yourself and your use of gesture are important too. Accentuate your key points through hand gestures. Keep them economical though – you do not want to be compared to an air stewardess as Andy once was by his cheeky Year 9s!

Feel Your Words

This might sound touchy-feely but it is really important. Completely passionless speech is dreary. You must instead put on the pretence that everything you say is of great importance. Where possible, you should aim to dig up the inherent emotion of your subject and create an atmosphere through your tone of voice. Never say, 'This is a bit boring but we've got to do it.' Teach everything as if it really matters and your students are more likely to believe so too, even if they do not always let on!

Repeat My Words

Ask students to repeat the main message of your explanation in their own words after you have finished. Target those with a track record of 'zoning out'. Putting them on the spot regularly will remind them to keep on track in future. You could also get them to tell you the first step they are going to take.

---

12 Michael Marland, *The Craft of the Classroom: A Survival Guide* (Oxford: Heinemann Books, 1975), pp. 73–74.

11. Use Razor-Sharp Instructions

How do I make sure students know exactly what it is I want them to do?

Instructions inform children what to do rather than what they need to understand. Incomplete or overcomplicated instructions may leave students thinking more about basic practicalities rather than the subject content they need to learn.

Some simple tips for honing your instructions include:

♦ Ensure that there is complete silence in the room, eyes are on you and all equipment is down before beginning. Be stubborn. Do not start until this is the case.

♦ Remind them that they are not to start working until you have finished speaking.

♦ Cut procedural instructions down into short, simple sequences. If you have any more than three or four points, consider breaking up the instructions into chunks so that they complete the first three before beginning on the next three.

♦ Start sentences with imperative verbs and use a firm tone: 'Start by …', 'Think about …', 'Make sure you …'

♦ If possible, ensure that instructions are also projected or written on the board.

♦ Field any questions.

♦ Ask a student or two to repeat the instructions again.

♦ Once started, alert the class to one or two who are following the instructions quickly and accurately with a simple, 'Thank you, Adam. Thank you, Tracy.'

12. Explain with Props and Supports

How can I use props and other supports to effectively support my explanations?

The worst explanations are often accompanied by over-detailed slide-shows. These sound and light extravaganzas can very easily dominate. They can also make you feel like you need to plough on relentlessly with your lesson, even if the class are not yet ready. At their worst, they are the enemy of subtle, responsive teaching. Children do not always respond as we expect them to. Thirty slides to fall back on can be comforting, but can too easily dictate and stand in the way of the adaption we might need to make.

Here are some ways teachers can use props and supports more effectively:

♦ Keep slides mainly for instructions, visual supports, models (see Chapter 3) and scaffolds to be used during practice (see Chapter 4). Use very few words on the slides. Keep them simple and if you do need to write a lot on them, give students a chance to read it before talking over the top.

♦ Slides can provide useful speaking cues during extended explanations. A good idea is to use animation features so that you can reveal cues one by one as you need them. In this way, your listeners do not read ahead or become swamped by a barrage of sentences.

♦ Aim to go naked! Teach a few lessons every week without a slide-show so that you can practise natural explanations and modelling. Use the board as much as possible – your notes are a step-by-step guide to your thinking. It is a wonderful way to model your thinking processes – notes allow students to look back if they forget something or lose attention for a moment.

♦ Bring in props and perform practical demonstrations whenever you can. So, in science – a subject where this strategy is often used – you could burn a piece of magnesium ribbon to form magnesium oxide to demonstrate that compounds are a completely different substance to the elements that formed them.

♦ Use pictures, images and diagrams to augment your explanations. For instance, it is much easier for the students to understand what Shakespearean theatre was like if you show them a picture of the Globe in London. (Even better, of course, is to take your classes to the theatre!)

13. Explain to Each Other

When are the best times for students to explain ideas to each other?

A well-known group-work strategy is to hand explanation rights over to the students in a technique known as home and expert groups. Students leave their home group to study a topic on the expert table, before all return to their home group to teach the rest what they have learnt on the expert table. By the close of the lesson, in beautiful symmetry, all students will have taught each other. Or so the theory goes …

Unfortunately there is a snag. Unlike their teachers, students are very rarely subject experts – if they were, what would be the point of teaching them in the first place? Despite the fact that such tasks might be engaging, many students will leave with sizeable gaps in their knowledge, particularly if they are being introduced to complex material for the first time.

We are not suggesting that students should never be asked to explain to one another or work collaboratively on new learning. We are arguing instead that this should usually happen *after* the key information has been explained by the teacher. Explaining their understanding in pairs or groups is an excellent strategy because it allows students to rephrase the new material in their own words, reflect on it and even critique and question it. Research suggests that elaboration – explaining why something is true by linking it to what you already know – is an effective way of helping students to remember new concepts.[13] Similarly, it is also useful for a child who understands a concept to explain it to another who is still uncertain. Indeed, any practice of subject-specific academic language that involves students talking together as a whole class, in small groups or pairs is beneficial. The key point, however, is that such approaches should supplement explicit teaching, not replace it.

13 John Dunlosky, Katherine A. Rawson, Elizabeth J. Marsh, Mitchell J. Nathan and Daniel T. Willingham, Improving Students' Learning with Effective Learning Techniques: Promising Directions from Cognitive and Educational Psychology, *Psychological Science in the Public Interest* 14(1) (2013): 4–58. Available at: http://www.indiana.edu/~pcl/rgoldsto/courses/ dunloskyimprovinglearning.pdf.

Evidence from the Education Endowment Foundation (EEF) suggest that peer tutoring, when students pair up to teach one another, is a very effective method if implemented carefully. It helps both the tutor and the tutee.[14] Findings reveal that one of the most effective methods is to take two classes from separate year groups (say Year 8 and Year 10) and pair up students according to ability. The strongest Year 10 should tutor the strongest Year 8, while the weakest Year 10 tutor the weakest Year 8. Once again, however, the EEF are at pains to point out that such schemes should support the teacher, not replace the teacher.

Student-to-student explanation activities, such as the home and expert group task, can be very successful, and we would advise you to try them. They are probably best utilised as ways to practise and develop knowledge and skills, rather than as ways to share new and challenging content for the first time.

14. Reflecting on Explanation

Why is explanation less fashionable than questioning and feedback?

Professional development in schools is rarely devoted to explanation as a discrete teaching strategy. Despite being an essential part of most lessons, and clearly crucial to student learning, it does not currently have the same kudos as general strategies such as questioning and feedback. One reason for this might be that a good explanation is inextricably linked to a teacher's subject knowledge, so it is hard to isolate its generic features from the specific content being taught.

---

14 See: https://educationendowmentfoundation.org.uk/toolkit/toolkit-a-z/peer-tutoring/.

Of course, the nature of the topic we are teaching will always dictate the way we choose to explain it. Each new explanation must match the nature and difficulty of the subject content with the relative proficiency and knowledge of the class. There are no neat, one-size-fits-all solutions. Nevertheless, our own experiences in the classroom have made it clear to us that the humble explanation is worthy of much closer inspection than it currently receives.

How much do students really learn from being spoken to by a teacher?

Maths teacher Lee Ridout tells a story from his student days. He was sitting in a huge lecture theatre as his professor, far off in the distance, addressed his audience of undergraduates. Lee and the others around him were expected to sit quietly and diligently take notes – interrupting your professor while he filled your mind with mathematical theorems was not the done thing!

One day Lee had had enough. He asked the people around him if they had any clue what the lecturer was going on about. They said no. Lee stood up, waving frantically: 'Excuse me, excuse me. I don't get it!' The professor was lost for words. A member of his audience had never interrupted him before. This memory is a fitting reminder for Lee on why he must always engage with his students, because if not, many of them may well be sitting listening to something they do not understand.

Even though this chapter argues for the importance of teacher talk, teaching must never be considered a performance or a show. It is an interactive art. When we talk, we talk to the children in front of us, not the back wall of the room.

How long should I explain for?

Once again there are no hard-and-fast rules. Some suggest that a teacher should never talk for more than ten minutes. This might be right during some lessons, but in other lessons it would be wrong. The same class will listen intently to one topic for fifteen minutes but lose focus after five minutes on another. Some students have poor skills of concentration whereas others listen carefully for extended periods. Often these differences are caused by the relative difficulty of the content and sometimes by contextual factors such as the time of day or, strangely enough, how windy it is outside!

The best teachers are responsive to classroom atmosphere and are constantly on the lookout for the subtle cues that students are not understanding or losing concentration. Some children are very good at hiding this; others make it fairly obvious by staring out of the window or putting their heads on their desks. While it is best to keep your explanations of complex concepts short and focused, it is not always necessary to do so. If a class can listen to a gripping story uninterrupted for an hour, they can listen to an interesting explanation for an extended period of time too.

Chapter 3
Modelling

Anya and Her History Essay

Anya is an ambitious Year 7 student. She has enjoyed learning about the Tudors and, as an end-of-term assessment, her history teacher has asked the class to write an essay based on Elizabeth I. Anya has studied a range of sources that shed light on Elizabeth's rule and feels confident that she has the knowledge to write a detailed essay. Her teacher shares the success criteria for a high standard essay with the class. These are: describe and begin to analyse the different types of events and change that occurred under Elizabeth's rule; understand that there were different types of causes to these events; suggest the most important cause; use sources of information to help reach and support a conclusion; describe and begin to explain different historical interpretations of Elizabeth and the events occurring during her reign.

The success criteria provide some useful information to help Anya with her essay, but only some. She knows that she needs to discuss a range of causes, make reference to sources and write a conclusion. But the reality is she does not know how. In fact, she has no understanding what an essay that 'analyses' historical events even looks like, let alone how to write one. Eventually, Anya puts all her effort into a long, detailed piece of writing. The final product is written in narrative form rather than in the discursive style of an academic historical essay. Although she tried to take heed of them, the success criteria were just too abstract to support Anya in any meaningful way.

Tim and His History Essay

In the classroom next door to Anya's, Tim has also studied Elizabeth I and will be completing the same task as Anya. Tim's teacher, Mr Carver, takes a different tack. Instead of sharing success criteria, Mr Carver has used the assessment criteria to write three exemplar paragraphs. Each of the paragraphs is written about the same topic – the influence that Elizabeth's staunch Protestantism had on her reign. Mr Carver has written one exemplar paragraph at a low level, one at a medium level and one at a high level.

Before Tim and his class begin writing their essays, Mr Carver shows them the exemplar paragraphs and gets the class to put them in the correct order – from best to worst. Mr Carver tells the class that they must aim to write their whole essay in the style of the best exemplar. He gives them a rough plan to work from – a writing frame – and sets them off. Tim fairs a little better than Anya, but struggles to maintain a suitable academic style across his essay.

Modelling –
What It Is And Why It Matters

Wrapped and packaged for our convenience, modern life serves up an endless supply of finished articles – think of television dramas, wedding cakes, hit singles or even city skyscrapers. It is easy to experience and enjoy these final products without considering the processes of design and construction that brought them to life.

From writing a poem to factoring an equation, from passing a rugby ball to designing a website, students in school are constantly in the process of creating products and performances. However, these do not reach a high standard by magic. They are always the result of combinations of procedures, some relatively simple, others extremely complex. As teachers, it is our responsibility to show students how to use and manipulate their knowledge to form these end products and, just as importantly, to ensure that they are of as high a standard as possible.

This is why modelling is such a vital element to teaching. To learn how to do something, students need to watch and listen to experts as they guide them through the process, step by step, before they make an attempt themselves. This also works in reverse through deconstruction. Students start by seeing an example of an end product and work backwards from there, carefully identifying and dissecting the stages and parts that, together, contribute to its overall quality and accuracy.

Let's go back to our two scenarios. In Anya's case, her teacher neither modelled nor deconstructed a history essay with the class. She was left like a ship without a rudder. As Anya had scant prior understanding of how her essay should be written, it is little wonder that she could not write one. In the second scenario, Tim's teacher recognised the need to show the students model paragraphs. What was missing, however, was any focused deconstruction or comparison of these three exemplars. Tim's teacher brushed over this. Seeing a high standard model is useful, of course, but not half as much as dismantling it and thinking about how the components work together.

Explanation and modelling are natural bedfellows. A history teacher might explain the causes of Hitler's rise to power and then model how to construct an evaluative essay on the topic. A maths teacher might explain the concept of long division while using the board to guide the class through the incremental stages. Good modelling, often aided by strong questioning and timely feedback, sends students on a journey towards independence, as exemplified below:

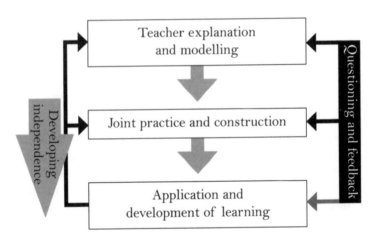

As discussed in Chapter 2, many in education are now beginning to question the fashionable notion of independent learning – the idea that we can facilitate instruction so that content is 'discovered' by students rather than passed from expert to novice. Researchers and educationalists have promoted the theory of the human social brain, one that has been shaped by evolution to learn from others, rather than to construct meaning itself.[1] Wherever the truth lies, we, along with all the practising teachers we have come across,

1   Hattie and Yates, *Visible Learning and the Science of How We Learn*, pp. 72–81.

can attest wholeheartedly to the effectiveness of the modelling process as the first step in a child's journey towards independence.

There are well-researched benefits too from studying worked examples and whole problems before they are tackled. Worked examples are successfully completed solutions that are introduced to students before they attempt similar problems themselves. Research has demonstrated that by studying worked examples prior to tackling new problems, students tend to perform better in later tests.[2] For example, in maths, students might study prepared solutions to quadratic equations before practising similar equations themselves.

Researchers and classroom teachers alike, as documented by Rosenshine, have found that modelling a procedure in small step-by-step chunks, followed by focused practice, followed by more modelling and practice, is a particularly effective teaching method, particularly when taking students through difficult tasks.[3]

There is, of course, a behavioural element to modelling too. You will not need us to remind you of the reciprocal nature of classroom behaviour. As teachers, whether we like it or not, we model everything. A calm voice can elicit calm behaviour in return; if we respectfully listen to our students, they are more likely to listen respectfully to us. Model a love of your subject and a belief that there is no glass ceiling to

---

2   Hattie and Yates, *Visible Learning and the Science of How We Learn*, pp. 151–152.
3   Rosenshine, Principles of Instruction.

success, and your students are more likely to believe this to be true.

We have found that there are two essentials to day-to-day modelling. The first is not to assume that students know how to do something they have never been taught how to do. The second is to always model high. It is through modelling that you set the benchmark for excellence.

1. Live Modelling

What is the most effective way to model written products?

The product students deliver most regularly in lessons is writing, yet we often expect them to write organically with little explicit guidance on the minute mechanics of the process. Anya and Tim's experiences are all too common. If there is a writing element to your curriculum, it should probably be modelled.

We heartily echo the following sentiment from US writing specialist Kelly Gallagher: 'of all the strategies I have learned in my twenty-five years of teaching, no strategy improves my students' writing more than having my students watch and listen to me as I write and think aloud. None.'[4]

Live writing is scripting a text at the front of the class, often with the help of students. It is a messy and stop-start affair which mirrors the thinking processes that support independent writing. Your students see you, an expert writer, in your subject domain, modelling the decision-making process that leads to a successful piece of writing. Many

---

4 Kelly Gallagher, *Write Like This: Teaching Real-world Writing Through Modelling and Mentor Texts* (Portland, ME: Stenhouse Publishers, 2011), p. 15.

unconscious habits – such as weighing up vocabulary choices, deliberating over sentence structure, editing brutally and proofreading with care – can then be made explicit to students who may never have thought in this way before.

Like all aspects of teaching, the more you practise live writing, the better you get at it. It has two key features: when you model independently and the students listen, and when the students take part in the process (sometimes known as co-construction). The latter will generally follow the former but the reality tends to be more organic – they work in tandem.

The following structure, which Andy uses for live writing, can be easily adapted to any live modelling of a target product, writing or otherwise:

♦ Your aim is to handwrite or type a short piece at the front of the class (a paragraph or two) that captures the academic register and structure suitable for proficient writing in your subject area.

♦ You might benefit from practising the piece prior to the lesson with a quick rough draft or listing a few key terms as cues in case you lose direction at any point.

♦ Make it clear to the class why you are doing this and what it is you expect students to learn from the process: 'We are going to be modelling x so that you will be able to do x yourselves.'

- Begin by modelling and writing out the first few sentences. Talk through your decisions and point out your successes – or 'call your shots' as Lemov, Woolway and Yezzi put it.[5] Do not fear indecision, mistakes and writer's block. Admit your struggles openly – students will appreciate this. You will then be modelling how to find solutions to the same obstacles the students will face when, a little later, they try it out for themselves.

- When you are ready, perhaps after the first sentence or two, allow the class to collaborate with you. You might start by asking, 'Which word would work best here?' before moving on to 'What should the next sentence focus on?' or 'How shall we link this new sentence to the previous one?' Encourage debate and negotiation. Even if the pace of modelling grinds to a halt, rich discussions about subject content and language are too good an opportunity to be missed.

- Modelling to a high standard and managing a class at the same time can be tricky! To keep students in order, you can ask them to copy the model down in their books. This is doubly useful as they can refer back to it later when working independently.

- When finished, ask students to critique and proofread the model with you, and then edit it together.

- Finally, ask them to 'call your shots': 'Remind me, Sam, why is this a successful paragraph?' You might want to use these points as the success criteria or a checklist of stages for the students to make use of in their subsequent pieces.

- It is easy to end these teaching sequences feeling slightly disheartened: they can lack fluency and structure. You should ignore your misgivings. Learning is hardly ever a fluent process.

---

5 Doug Lemov, Erica Woolway and Katie Yezzi, *Practice Perfect: 42 Rules for Getting Better at Getting Better* (San Francisco, CA: Jossey-Bass, 2012), p. 81.

It is important that time is built in for students to work independently directly after modelling so they can practise the new techniques. If students are using visible scaffolds or stimuli (e.g. key word lists, memory cues, thesauruses, ticklists) be sure to model how to use these during the live sequence.

An interesting variant on this strategy is to film yourself completing a problem with a pen and paper. As you play this to the class, you can pause regularly and rewind back through the steps. It is easy to reuse with different classes and could even be uploaded to YouTube for students to watch at home.

A second variant that Andy often uses is to write a very poor example in advance of the lesson – one containing the weaknesses and misconceptions common to that particular class or topic. He then uses the live modelling time to improve on it. This technique is also a useful way to model the editing process.

A more nuanced approach to Live Modelling is to partially assume the role of the novice yourself. Before you begin, try to second-guess the setbacks students will face and the emotional anxieties these might lead to. From this position, guide students towards strategies that will help them to overcome these sticky points:

I must say, when I first looked at this problem I didn't know where to start. And then it hit me that I should …

It's okay to feel frustrated at this point. I often do. Now the best way to solve this is to …

I always used to struggle with …, but when I started to use this strategy I found it much easier.

Notice how these phrases help you not only to model products and processes, but also how to persevere in the face of doubt and worry, and that struggle is a key element of learning. If you show your students your empathy, they will usually respond by taking more risks.

2. Prepare in Advance

Should I always model in front of the class, or are there advantages to completing a model in advance?

There are some advantages to designing models prior to lessons – the 'Here's one I made earlier' approach. Although students will not witness real-time construction (as in Live Modelling), you have more time to fine-tune the model and prepare accompanying questions and explanations in advance.

A teacher-generated model has the benefit of being bespoke. You can design it to perfectly match the needs of the class with the assessment criteria. You can model a whole product (e.g. an essay, a mathematical problem, a crusty loaf of bread) or you can micro-model a key part (e.g. a paragraph, a particular working-out, the perfect bread dough).

By creating a model in advance, you are compelled to see the task through the eyes of your students before the lesson. This means you can nip in the bud any potential misconceptions and pre-empt any potential icebergs that students could run aground on. It is vital, however, that these exemplars are carefully deconstructed with the class in mind. Remember Tim and his history essay? Students must be made aware of the component parts and how they fit together, otherwise an exemplar can prove more daunting than useful.

Take this exemplar paragraph that Andy created based on Seamus Heaney's poem, 'Mid-Term Break':

Once the awkwardness is over it is replaced by an overwhelming numbness. The boy shows little emotion when he describes his mother's 'angry tearless sighs'. When the body arrives it is described as a 'corpse'. This is a medical term, and it is a peculiarly clinical way to describe your brother who has tragically just passed away. Perhaps it suggests that the narrator is still unable to come to terms with what has happened and, at this stage, is unable to feel anything at all.

Andy guided his students towards identifying the following successful features:

- The first sentence (the topic sentence) refers back to the previous paragraph, which was about awkwardness, and forward into this one, about numbness.

- The writer uses short, embedded quotations – 'angry tearless sighs' and 'corpse'.

- The effect of the word 'corpse' is analysed in detail.

- The last sentence is made into a tentative assertion about the writer's emotions through the word 'perhaps'.

The class were able to use both the model and the criteria they had unearthed in their subsequent work.

A key consideration is the degree of separation between the model and the target product. In other words, you need to consider the work the students will be completing after interacting with a model. In the above example, it would have been pointless for them to have written another paragraph on the same verse of the poem – that would merely be a test of remembering or copying! It is far better for the students either to write the next paragraph of the Heaney essay focusing on another of the boy's emotions or to write about emotions in another poem using the same writing strategy. If how and where the learning will be transferred are not carefully thought through, modelling becomes a copying exercise, actively preventing any independent thought.

3. Admire Each Other

Should models and exemplars be created only by the teacher?

Self-efficacy is a concept from psychology first introduced by Albert Bandura in the 1970s.[6] It refers to the real-time belief that we can succeed in the task we are currently attempting. There are a broad range of complex factors at work that influence this judgement; however, for the purposes of this chapter the most important is the influence of a realistic role model.

This is why the regular use of student-generated models and demonstrations is such a powerful lever. A teacher-generated model has been designed by you, a relative expert. A student-generated model, however, has been created by someone your students can relate to, someone of the same

---

6   Albert Bandura, Self-Efficacy: Towards a Unifying Theory of Behaviour Change, *Psychological Review* 84(2) (1977): 191–215. Available at: http://www. uky.edu/~eushe2/Bandura/Bandura1977PR.pdf.

age and social group, sitting in the same room. It might be the boy picking his nose right next to you. It might be the girl from two years ago whose initials are still etched on your desk. Either way, a child is much more likely to believe that they can emulate excellent examples if they can identify with their creators. A student watching the performance of a peer in a dance lesson might think, 'Like me, they have only just started to learn to dance. If they can attempt and succeed with a pirouette, I probably can too.'[7] However, be careful. If the model reveals skill way beyond the child's current capability, confidence might be shattered.

There are plenty of ways you can get students to be inspired by the success of their peers:

♦ If possible share a 'Here's one I made earlier' teacher model alongside past-student exemplar work. Compare the two and let them shed light on one another. Even better, get students to identify how the student model trumps the teacher one – a task most classes participate in with glee!

♦ Regularly pause lessons to read out and exhibit great examples of work from around the class. Make sure you or the students 'call the shots' by identifying the success-ful features of the piece.

♦ Introduce magpie learning. Find opportunities for stu-dents to circulate and read each other's work – not just to peer assess, but to borrow thoughts and ideas that they can use to improve their own work. Why not reserve a few pages of students' exercise books at the start of the year for them to write down these rich pickings?

♦ Set aside decent periods of time for students to browse through collections and anthologies of former students' work, or take them on a trip to the Gallery of Excellence (see Chapter 1).

---

7   Hattie and Yates, *Visible Learning and the Science of How We Learn*, pp. 219–223.

- Photograph work on an iPad or visualiser and show it to the whole class while students are working. Discuss it and consider its strengths and weaknesses. In practical lessons, use video footage of students at work in the same manner. You will need to consider two factors carefully: the quality of the piece and the feelings of the student whose work is being presented. A kind and trusting class-room ethos is most important here.

- Deconstruct not only the knowledge and skill demon-strated in exemplars, but also the learning behaviours and metacognitive strategies on show. What do you think they did when she got stuck? Can you see how they edited their work to improve it? How did they use their plan to assist them? Would this kind of accuracy have been pos-sible if they had spent the lesson turning around and talking to their mates?

- Keep copies of each draft of the work of a student who has made particularly impressive progress. Use these to model the journey to success – from the flawed first draft to the beautiful final piece – with your next class. (See Ron Berger's YouTube video on the story of 'Austin's Butterfly' for a great example of this.[8])

You must ensure that the expertise exhibited in the model work is achievable, at least in part, for all. Models can back-fire: when they are too challenging, they can even decrease motivation by making success seem impossible. For some, however, models should present challenges to be surpassed, which is why critiquing all models, even high standard ones, is so important. No work should be considered perfect. Everything can be improved.

You can also ask students to model to one another. If one student has produced, or is producing, a strong piece of work using an effective method and another needs extra support, it makes sense to pair them up. Although you should not rely on students to do your teaching for you, they

---

8   See http://www.youtube.com/watch?v=hqh1MRWZjms.

often have the knack for remodelling in a language that their peers intuitively understand.

One final strategy is to model the journey. At the beginning of each academic year, identify a student who made great progress in your class the previous year and then show examples of their work from across the year, narrating the student's journey. (Note the similarity with the Become a Storyteller strategy from Chapter 2.)

Here are two pieces that exemplify the progress a Year 10 student made in Andy's English group, both written about Steinbeck's *Of Mice and Men*. The first example is from October:

George was in disbelief as he sat 'stiffly' on the bank, he was frozen with shock. He also 'looked at his right hand that had thrown the gun away,' this means that he was emotionaly [sic] numb. It may also suggest that he was angry at what his 'right hand' just did, it shot his friend. It shows that he wanted to blame it on something. Steinbeck used these words to replicate how frightened he was after he shot Lennie.

And the second is from June:

Furthermore, she reveals a more dominant side when she stands 'over him'. Here Steinbeck describes physical levels to illustrate social hierarchy. To emphasise her power, Steinbeck uses the metaphor 'whip', a harsh sounding word that not only stings Crooks but the reader as they feel his pain. This onomatopoeic word generates images of slavery, which was abollished [sic] many years before, yet is still remembered to this day. Hence, we could speculate that Steinbeck felt a certain degree of sympathy for Crooks. Moreover, it conjures up images of a slave master, Curley's Wife and Crooks, the slave. It is this that gives Curley's Wife a vociferous tone. When Crooks had 'reduced himself' to nothing', our sympathy is eroded away from Curley's Wife and deposited into Crooks. On closer analysis, it might seem that by describing Curley's Wife as powerful, he is actually exposing her weakness as Crooks is the only person she feels she can attack.

Sharing such exemplars can give genuine credibility to abstract notions like success, progress and improvement. The teenage writer of these paragraphs worked diligently all year, never giving up, always seeking small gains and winning small victories. Over time, these accumulatively led to genuine, measureable academic success.

A further illustration of this strategy came from the beginning of last academic year when Shaun watched Gail Christie, a very accomplished art teacher, as she introduced her new GCSE class to the A* sketchbook of a former student. A hushed awe fell on the room as Gail leafed through the book, pointing out the ways this student's technique and creativity had matured over the two-year course. This strategy, which can be adjusted to fit any subject, is a wonderfully powerful way to put in place challenging – yet still obtainable – expectations right from day one.

4. Grow Expert Apprenticeships

Should we look beyond the walls of our school to find models and exemplars?

Even though you should exercise caution when sharing extremely high expertise models, you should not forget how inspiring and motivating phrases like the following can be:

Here's a clip of Cristiano Ronaldo scoring a wonderful free kick. Now I am going to show you how to connect with the ball like he did.

Have a nibble of Nigella Lawson's favourite chocolate cake. In ten steps, you will be able to make a replica one yourself.

Let's read the opening chapter to Jack London's White Fang. *Your aim is to write as well as London himself.*

Once again, ample time must be devoted to the careful unpicking of such models with the class. The aim is to shed light on the pivotal actions and procedures that make the models tick. To do this, look for the simple answers to seemingly difficult processes without understating the skill level required. Might it be the angle of Ronaldo's run-up? Could it be Nigella's careful use of cocoa powder? Is it the way London personifies nature through his use of verbs?

It is unrealistic to expect a class of 14-year-olds to become world-beating superstars within the space of an hour's lesson. Our point is more subtle than this. Nevertheless, in the attempt to emulate experts, students may well go further than they would have if they had not had a go in the first place. With careful breaking down and lots of practice, even the most audacious challenges are more achievable than we first imagine.

When Andy used the phrase from above about London's *White Fang* with his Year 8 English class in preparation for writing their Benchmark Brilliance (see Chapter 1) he had the following plan of action:

1   Read the first three chapters of *White Fang* to engage with the themes and storyline.

2   Hone in on successful sentence structures used by London and what makes them effective.

3   Identify how London creates personification through verb and adjective choice.

Thus his class closely dissected London's sentences before they practised writing their own in a similar style. Here is a sample paragraph, written by a 13-year-old boy, of the quality of writing that this process eventually resulted in:

Where light had been mere minutes before, darkness began to close in. Staring out into the unfathomable depths of shadow, the men huddled for warmth. They watched as the shadows around them stretched and distorted, finally overtaken altogether. Lying by the fire, the dogs were dopey, just barely awake, ears perked, falsely alert. Suddenly, one of the dogs sprang to life, only to fall and be dragged backwards into the unknown realm of the night. Gleaming eyes floated on a lead black backdrop and the low hum of growling shot tendrils of fear up the men's spines. Sparks rose from the fire, giving lit glimpses of the night. A gust buffeted snow onto the fire, and the mirthless wind plunged them into darkness.

The night was whole once again.

If you are prepared to put time into the close deconstruction of expert models – or mentor texts as they are sometimes known – the results, like the one above, can be pleasantly surprising. Similarly, inviting in experts from different fields to present to and work with students is a popular way to widen horizons.

5. Share Multiple Models

Is one model always enough?

Huge benefits can be mined from using more than one model to exemplify a solution or procedure. In many subjects, various problems might appear structurally different, even though they have the same deep structure and can be solved using an identical strategy. This is particularly so in subjects like science and maths. In physics, for example, to help students master a formula such as acceleration = change in speed / time taken, the teacher can model how to solve a number of problems such as, calculating acceleration from a velocity/time graph, calculating the acceleration of a trolley moving down a slope using a ticker tape timer and calculating acceleration from a written question.

In each of these examples, the teacher will be modelling not only how to solve a problem using the formula, but also the thinking process that helps a proficient mathematician to transfer the knowledge from one situation to another seemingly unrelated situation. Cognitive scientist Daniel Willingham suggests that this comparison method may help students to see the 'deep structure' behind problems and so assist with the transfer of knowledge from one context to another.[9]

Multiple modelling works differently in other subject areas. Displaying two models of differing quality side by side and comparing them is another popular method. High quality and poor quality are easier to spot in relief. Take these introductory paragraphs to a geography case study:

Model 1

The River Ganges flows from Uttarakhand in the Western Himalayas, through the Gangetic plain of North India and Bangladesh, until it empties into the Bay of Bengal. The third largest river in the world, the Ganges provides water and washing facilities for the millions of Indians who live along its banks. Not only is it a life source, but it is also considered sacred and worshipped as the goddess Ganga by India's Hindu population. In recent times, however, industrial waste and non-biodegradable religious offerings have led to the river becoming the seventh most polluted in the world.

---

9 Willingham, *Why Don't Students Like School?*, pp. 102–103.

Model 2

The River Ganges is in India and it is very polluted. It flows from India to Bangladesh and there are many religious offerings floating down the river. The mountains the river comes from are the Himalaya's where you will find Mount Everest. There is a lot of industrial waste in the river.

Model 1 is clearly more sophisticated than Model 2. As always, it is crucial to guide students towards understanding why one is stronger than the other (otherwise they might focus solely on the difference in quantity). For example:

♦ Model 1 uses a descriptive topic sentence to carefully delineate geographical facts, whereas Model 2 jumps straight into a discussion of pollution.

♦ Model 1 is structured carefully so that it moves from the beneficial effects of the river to the modern complication of pollution, whereas Model 2 misses out the beneficial effects. It is, therefore, more evaluative in style.

♦ Model 1 uses academic discursive markers – 'not only', 'in recent times, however' – whereas Model 2 is over-simplistic in its language use with no development of ideas.

We should again consider the degree of separation between the exemplar and the final product. The two exemplars would be perfect to use in a study of the River Nile, rather than the Ganges. The students would then write about the Nile in the same style as Model 1.

Multiple modelling can also inspire creativity. In subjects such as art and English, which often involve handing over artistic licence to students, sharing more than one model allows us to demonstrate that successful outcomes might be very different. If, for instance, students are about to sketch a self-portrait in charcoal, show them three very different excellent examples completed during an identical task set for a previous class. Similarly, if students are about to write a horror story, get them to compare three Gothic genre opening paragraphs from writers such as Edgar Allan Poe and Charles Dickens. Three is a perfect number to share. Guide students towards the unique qualities that help each piece of work to stand out, but also the common qualities exhibited by all.

6. Be a Machine Gun Modeller

How do I involve my class in the modelling process?

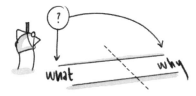

In the very best practical lessons we have witnessed – in subjects such as art, PE and science – the most effective modelling goes hand in hand with quick-fire questioning. Teachers physically show the students what to do but punctuate their demonstrations with many questions on the finer detail of the technique they are exemplifying. Questions ensure that students are listening and that common misconceptions can be quickly cleared up.

The two most important questions are:

1   The descriptive question: what am I doing?

2   The explanatory question: why am I doing it?

Take the PE teacher who is modelling to his students how to throw a javelin and breaking up his explanation with probing questions:

How am I gripping the javelin? Tell me what my fingers are doing ... Tom?

Why am I gripping it this way ... Holly?

How would you describe my run-up ... Donna?

Why did I fully extend my front leg on release ... Tyler?

Many teachers will also deepen students' understanding by modelling common misunderstandings and misconceptions:

Why will the javelin go further if I release it from this point rather than that point ... Leslie?

What are the dangers of holding it like this ... Rashid?

You will notice that the questions finish with a short pause before the teacher selects a student. In this way, any student may be called on at any point, so all are expected to listen and mentally rehearse how they would answer.

A further option is to elect a student to play the 'model', freeing up the teacher to ask the questions while the student demonstrates. This is a common strategy in maths lessons and works particularly well after the teacher has initially modelled how to complete a procedure or solve a problem. A student is called to the front to re-model while the teacher questions the rest of the class: what should they do first? Have they got it right? What change do they need to make? Where to next? This strategy is doubly useful as the students get to see the process modelled more than once – by the teacher *and* the student.

7. Show Them How to Speak

As well as products and procedures, what else should I be modelling every day?

Many socially disadvantaged children have no access to academic oral language anywhere but in our classrooms, so it is a moral imperative that you exemplify the language you expect them to use. If you don't, who will? You should model Standard English at all times and students should be immersed in it from the off. In the same way, you should not avoid using subject-specific academic vocabulary early on, but embrace and encourage it. In science, a teacher might use 'viscous' instead of 'thick' straight away, and an English teacher might abolish the use of unsophisticated adjectives like 'nice' and 'good' and 'bad' and replace them with more subtle alternatives. Regular repetition will ensure that these terms soon become a part of students' working vocabulary, but if left too late it will be harder for them to adopt it.

Not all students will make the necessary inference that they should attempt to emulate the sophistication of your verbal utterings. Indeed, for an adolescent, 'sounding like sir' is not usually considered a socially desirable attribute! Therefore, we need to find ways of making our expectations clear. One solution comes at the planning stage. Before any form of student talk, we should plan in time for modelling.

Imagine students have been asked to explain their understanding of the causes of the Cold War in a history lesson:

In a moment I am going to ask a few of you to explain the causes of the Cold War. I'll start by giving you an example of the quality of answer I expect: 'One of the causes of the Cold War was the Soviet Union's historical relationship with the US and Britain. In 1918, the two countries had attempted to end the Russian Revolution and this memory created long-term resentment among the Soviet leadership.' You'll notice that I spoke in full sentences, gave a clear reason and used specific historical facts. Now, Tim, could you give me another reason in this style?

We may need to use questions to scaffold Tim's verbal response. The bar, however, has clearly been set. There is a simple rule of thumb: before any student talk – to the whole class or peer to peer – we must make performance expectations crystal clear. This is particularly true in the early weeks of the academic year. If, for instance, students are to deliver a presentation, then the teacher should have primed the class with a model presentation beforehand.

For discussions, a dummy run is useful:

Teacher: Kathy, what do you think is Macbeth's main motive for killing Duncan?

Kathy: Because he wanted to keep his wife happy.

Teacher: John?

John: I think it was his ambition to become king.

Teacher: Both of your points are great. Now let's think about how to conduct a discussion. Kathy, could you rephrase what you said into a full sentence.

Kathy: Macbeth's main motive for murdering King Duncan was because he wanted more than anything to keep Lady Macbeth happy.

Teacher: Now, John, could you speak to Kathy and explain why you are challenging her.

John: I disagree with you, Kathy, because although Macbeth obviously loves his wife, his desire to become king is even stronger.

Teacher: Develop that, John.

John: We see this at the moment he first meets the witches when Banquo states that he is 'rapt' by their prophesies.

Teacher (to the rest of the class): How did John and Kathy improve their discussion, and what does that tell you about how I expect our discussion to run today?

If you are wondering why all this is important, consider David Didau's theory: 'If you can say it, you can write it.'[10] If you follow this line of thinking, oral work directly feeds into the quality of student thinking and written work.

But what if speaking in formal, subject-specific language is not our strong point? As in Live Modelling, we should capitalise on our own shortcomings and model self-correction. Imagine you are a PE teacher explaining how to hit a cricket shot to a young batsman: 'You need to put your leg forward and hit the ball over there ... No, let me explain that in cricketing terms. You need to put your front foot forward and drive the ball through the off-side.'

8. Design a Feedback Mirror

Are there any advantages to presenting models after students have completed the work?

---

10 David Didau, *The Secret of Literacy: Making the Implicit Explicit* (Carmarthen: Independent Thinking Press, 2014), p. 83.

You are all set for a thrilling date. Your first impressions of the man you are to meet this evening at an Italian restaurant in town are more than encouraging. Quite frankly, he's hot! You must get everything right. You check your make-up in the mirror for the one-hundredth time …

In fact, the mirror is giving you immediate cosmetic feedback to compare against your conception of how your make-up, when applied to perfection, should look. You can immediately act on this feedback – leave it in place or touch it up once more. Remember, only you are the expert in how your mascara should look.

In other fields, however, we are novices and do not have an accurate or complete mental picture to fall back on. If the flush mechanism fails to work on a toilet at home, you might seek feedback by looking at the mechanism of another toilet in the house or search for a picture on the internet. You will compare the two and use this feedback to plan your next move. You search for useful feedback by making comparisons with models all the time in your everyday life.

You can easily bring this powerful effect into the classroom. After completing, say, a practice exam question, you can ask students to compare their piece against a good exemplar. They can then edit, redraft or set themselves targets for their next attempt. This approach works particularly well in practical subjects, such as art and DT, which by their nature are built around the creation of products: 'Compare your model bridge to the model I have here, and then go back to your desks to refine your design.' In drama, PE and other performance related subjects, students can compare video clips of themselves with video models.

This approach provides a potentially richer, quicker and more detailed form of feedback than a written comment. It is also a fantastically efficient time-saving method if you are particularly busy and want to give feedback quickly. Andy will often create a feedback model while the students are working. Sometimes he will show them the model later as a feedback instrument. Students compare their piece with his and then go away and improve their own. At other times, to provide students with more scaffolding, he will briefly reveal parts of his model as the class are working or talk them through how he has worked around a difficult sticking point.

9. Model the Kitchen Sink!

Should we model everything?

All teachers are acutely aware of the variance in student prior knowledge, yet Graham Nuthall's extraordinary research has illuminated just how extreme these differences are. Around a third of an individual student's learning is unique to them and is not learnt by others in the same class-room.[11] This finding has profound implications on the assumptions we make about what students already know and can do and what they do not know and cannot do.

Avoiding the 'they should already know that' trap is the first step. Blaming the child for not understanding something is entirely counterproductive. Instead, we must model all parts of the learning journey, however small and seemingly insignificant, whether they are summatively assessed or not. Note-taking, annotation, skim-reading, underlining the date and title, graph-drawing, editing, proofreading, redrafting, asking questions, answering questions, reading a textbook, planning extended writing, holding a tennis racket, peer assessment, mixing paints, drawing a timeline – all will benefit from modelling. If students are expected to use a worksheet or resource, show them how to do it. Otherwise, they may be challenged by simple practicalities (e.g. Where do I write my answer?) rather than by all-important subject content.

---

11 Nuthall, *The Hidden Lives of Learners*, p. 154.

You will, however, need to stay aware of your ultimate goal – that students will one day be able to do these things independently. When providing support, always consider how you will remove this scaffolding at a later date. You do not want to create a dependency culture.

One of your main focuses should be metacognition. Put simply, this is the way students plan, monitor and evaluate their own thinking as they are learning. Do not just expect all students to know how to organise their notes, plan an essay, respond to feedback or proofread their work. Instead, live model the planning process from your position of expertise or provide multiple exemplars of plans written by other students. Remember, too, that these processes might be very different depending on the subject. If you are a maths teacher, for instance, model how mathematicians check their workings out. The way you do this will be very different to how work is proofread in other subjects.

Finally, in the run-up to final exams, be sure to model how to approach exam questions. Many marks are lost in the exam hall not through students' lack of knowledge or insufficient revision, but because they lack a shrewd game plan. So, project an image of an exam paper on the board, talk through each question and explain what you would do if it was you who was sitting the exam. How would you ensure that you had interpreted the question accurately? What would be your first step? How would you bleed out every mark possible from the question? What would you do if you came upon a particularly hard question? How would you time yourself? Talk them through and model your thinking – this time as an expert passer of exams.

10. Archive Excellence

How can we inspire a 'modelling culture' in our schools and subject departments?

Models are among the most powerful of teaching resources. Part of our job as teachers is to track down, categorise and store these golden nuggets for the future. So much wonderful work is sadly consigned to the rubbish tip at the end of the academic year – work that could inspire the students and teachers of the future. We should seek to prevent this. The exemplars we collect should range from teacher-designed models, to student work, to those created by real-world experts in our subject areas.

Ron Berger sums up this sentiment beautifully: 'One of my jobs as a teacher, I feel, is to be an historian of excellence, an archiver of excellence.'[12]

Here are some tips on how to collect examples of students' work.

♦ Use tablets and smartphones to photograph work regularly. Save these on cloud storage applications such as Dropbox and folders that all teachers can access.

---

12 Berger, *An Ethic of Excellence*, p. 29.

- Create yearly anthologies and collections of the best student work across key stages and subject areas. Make sure these are disseminated to all staff.

- Host regular events to celebrate excellent work, and keep photo and video records of these occasions.

- Use displays to ensure that students are immersed in good examples.

- Ring-fence five to ten minutes of department meeting time for the sharing and comparing of excellent work.

- Team up with other local schools to share and compare excellent work.

- Create exemplar 'banks' to benchmark standards against grade boundaries. These are vital for staff and students alike; they transform abstract grade descriptors into concrete products that will influence the next generation.

Sadly, the average teacher often only comes face to face with the work produced in the classes of her colleagues during moderation meetings. The focus here becomes the accuracy of summative grades rather than the teaching that led to such work. This is a missed opportunity. Student work should not be considered as just the end product, an afterthought or a culmination of teaching practice. If we work backwards from the best student examples produced in our subjects, it not only becomes easier to map the journey to excellence for future cohorts, but it also becomes easier to challenge them to go one step further than the excellence of their predecessors.

Reflective Questions

Can modelling constrain creativity and independence?

Modelling is fundamental in stimulating and inspiring creativity. At its best, it gives students the tools they need to guide them towards independent mastery of the skills and procedures necessary for success in your subject area. But it has a dark side. When crudely implemented, it has the potential to restrict and narrow thinking rather than inspire it. Bad modelling can be akin to spoon-feeding; if it over-dominates it can lead to the teacher doing the cognitive work that the student should be doing themselves. This is why it is so important to regularly put models to one side and allow students to struggle for themselves. Exactly when to do this depends on the needs of your class and the individuals within it – your gut instinct will play a huge role.

There are a number of traps we advise you to watch out for. The first is to be careful that your models do not inhibit your most proficient students. Make sure you use a range of exemplars – as we suggested in the Share Multiple Models strategy – to show students that there is usually more than one way of approaching the same task. Discuss with the class why you are showing a model and how to get the best out of the process. If you only have time to introduce one exemplar, make sure that you also discuss alternative approaches to the same task.

The second concerns the modelling of extended writing. Make sure that students do not copy the model. Even if, as we suggest, you have planned in a degree of separation between the model and the final piece, some students will find any opportunity to crudely shoehorn ideas from the model into their own work. One way of avoiding this is to get students to plan their work independently before they see a model. In this way, the ideas are already in place, so the model gives guidance on how to manipulate the content but does not dictate it.

Third, remember that models do not replace knowledge. It is no use modelling an exam answer if students do not have the required knowledge to answer it. You are better off returning to the content first.

Should I model during every lesson?

Consider the main aim of modelling. You hope that your students will take up the mantle and, over time and through varying contexts, internalise the models you share with them. This means they not only replicate the key features when asked to, but also manipulate and adapt this knowledge in new contexts when necessary. You must be realistic and remember that, despite your high expectations, not all will manage this on the first, second, third ... or even the sixty-third attempt!

As a result, we have found it useful to think of modelling as a cycle. This helps you to account for the spacing effect (see Mix It Up in Chapter 4), which demonstrates what many teachers have always known intuitively: students need to keep coming back to material in spaced intervals if they are not to forget the knowledge and skills they have acquired. It might seem counterintuitive, but we should be wary of short-term gains won through great modelling. Just because a student has managed to successfully solve a challenging calculus problem after being exposed to a model or worked example, does not mean they will be able to repeat the feat next week, next month or next year. This is where practice, and if necessary, repeat modelling are required.

The strategies in this book are there to be combined. Cast your mind back to the Give Multiple Examples strategy in Chapter 2. To successfully learn how to write like a historian, a child might need a smorgasbord of modelling and explanation strategies over time – for example, live writing, comparative models, oral modelling and feedback mirrors. Since forgetting and misunderstanding are part and parcel of human nature, modelling a new skill once is rarely enough. Likewise, it would be unwise to consider modelling as a panacea to the complex range of genetic, environmental and motivational factors that have an impact on learning. It does, however, make a huge difference to many.

How do I ensure that models are carefully pitched to meet student needs?

Consider your models as another way to provide feedback. Once you know a class well, create models or choose exemplars that closely pinpoint the needs of your class. For example, if you know that in their last extended writing task your English class struggled to incorporate interesting adjectives convincingly into their work, make sure this problem is addressed in the exemplars you produce for the next task.

What about the varying needs within the same class? A shrewd ploy is to target questions during the deconstruction process. If you know, for instance, that Dan starts most of his sentences with pronouns and Esmee is prone to apostrophe errors, focus your attention on them:

Dan, can you find me two sentences that do not start with pronouns? How do they change the effect of the piece?

Esmee, can you explain why we have used an apostrophe here but not here?

At what point should we stop modelling and allow students complete independence?

Students will only master the knowledge and skills you teach them by spending lots of time practising. Infinitely more time should be spent on student practice than on the modelling that precedes it (practice is the subject of Chapter 4). You should also be mindful of the need to remove models and scaffolds regularly to allow students to make mistakes. These mistakes will inform both you and the students about where they need to go next and the content it would be wise to repeat.

Even so, this does not mean that you should stop the modelling process. If, in geography, students can now interpret a map independently, you should crank up the level of difficulty once more and model how to do this at A* standard and beyond. We should not forget that even those who excel academically at secondary school are still relative novices in comparison to the experts of the adult world.

Chapter 4
Practice

Year 9 Science

It has come to the end of half-term and it is time for your Year 9 science class to sit their end-of-unit test. You feel you have taught energy and electricity well. You know the content of the topic inside out and you have worked away into the small hours refining your lessons prior to their delivery. You have packed every moment with detailed modelling and concise explanation.

As the test ends, you collect the papers in eagerly; you desperately want to see the progress your students have made, the fruits of your labour. But when you read the answers, hopeful anticipation is swiftly overtaken by despair. Half the students appear to have forgotten everything! Some have not even attempted to lay pen to paper! The other half of the group have given the test a shot, yet basic misconceptions are rife. 'Why don't they just listen to me?' you ask desperately. Or in the worst moments, 'What makes me such a bad teacher?'

Amy

Amy is a great Year 11 student. She is polite, hard-working and hands in her homework punctually. She is motivated and clearly wants to do well in her English GCSE. The problem is that she seems unable to write a grammatical sentence. Sentences run into each other and she appears to believe that the inclusion of a main verb is an optional extra. Time and time again you repeat your concerns to her, but still she makes the same mistake. Eventually you settle on an answer to Amy's problem: through some quirk of nature or nurture, Amy is predisposed to being unable to write a grammatical sentence. You will just have to accept it. And so will she.

Practice – What It Is And Why It Matters

Both of us have regularly experienced the above scenarios and they have their roots in the same issue: a lack of rigorous and structured practice. Because they have had little time to practise the new material, the conscientious science teacher's students are unable to retain the knowledge they have been painstakingly fed. He has assumed that by exposing students to lots of new knowledge his class will remember and apply it. Unsurprisingly, teaching is much more than explanation and modelling.

In the second scenario, Amy has not suffered from a lack of practice per se, but from a lack of good practice. Repeated practice, good or bad, leads inevitably to habits that occur with little or no conscious thought – something psychologists refer to as 'automaticity'. It is such a hard job to help Amy reverse her grammatical slip-ups because they have become as much a part of her unthinking behaviour as brushing her teeth in the morning or tying up her shoelaces.

In *Practice Perfect*, Doug Lemov, Erica Woolway and Katie Yezzi argue that 'practice makes permanent' or, to put it another way, the quality of knowledge and performance our students retain is dependent on the quality of practice they put in. In the words of Graham Nuthall, students 'learn what they do'[1] – just like Amy has. Our task is to shape learning so that simple misconceptions and misunderstandings do not become immovable.

The basic premise of this chapter is that you should provide students with the time they need to practise new material, and that this practice should be careful, deliberate and just outside of the child's comfort zone (see Chapter 1). Important, too, is that this practice achieves a high degree of accuracy – in the words of American football legend Vince Lombardi, 'Practice does not make perfect. Only *perfect* practice makes perfect.'

In *Bounce*, writer and former British table tennis champion Matthew Syed has written about how he owes his own sporting success to a mixture of luck and practice rather than innate talent.[2] A combination of favourable factors from the context of his upbringing conspired favourably to his advantage, such as the fact that he attended a school that just so happened to have a top quality table tennis coach as a PE teacher. From here, Syed's path to table tennis prowess was determined by his practice regimes, which were helped by top quality coaching, facilities and training schedules. Syed shows that the lightning quick reflexes of a table tennis player are learnt behaviour, not the result of God-given natural ability. Drawing on research into deliberate practice by psychologist K. Anders Ericsson, Syed's book promotes the power of practice and its relevance to a wide range of fields – from chess, to violin playing, to fire-fighting … to our classrooms.

---

1   Nuthall, *The Hidden Lives of Learners*, p. 36.
2   Matthew Syed, *Bounce: The Myth of Talent and the Power of Practice* (London: Fourth Estate, 2011).

Ostensibly, the message is exciting. If we can design the best conditions for practice in our classrooms, we will have a greater impact on long-term student progress. But there is a snag. Good conditions for practice must be coupled with effort and motivation on the students' part. A student who understands the pay-off of hard work is likely to forge opportunities for meaningful practice even with the least effective teacher; conversely, a student who is unwilling to put in the sweat and tears will make little progress even if the practice climate is perfect. Once again, it comes back to the growth mindset. Genuine mastery of a challenging task is impossible without effort.

Broadly speaking, we consider two types of practice. The first is *practice for fluency*. By fluency, we are referring to knowledge and procedures so well-consolidated in the child's long-term memory that they can be effortlessly recalled or performed once mastered. They do not place any pressure on the 'thinking space' in the child's mind – the working memory – and so can be brought to mind swiftly and easily.[3]

The knowledge that forms the bedrock of your subject should be practised to fluency. In geography, this might be the fact that the Atlantic Ocean separates Europe and America; in maths, that $7 \times 7 = 49$; in English, that a metaphor is a figure of speech that suggests a resemblance between unrelated objects. Once known, the child can move on to using this knowledge to think about something more

---

3   See Willingham, *Why Don't Students Like School?*

challenging; however, without this fluency, lack of knowledge will hamper future progression. Consider asking students to think about Shakespeare's use of imagery when they have not yet mastered what a metaphor is. This dearth of basic knowledge will make it harder for a child to move on to more sophisticated interpretations.

The second type is *deliberate practice*. This is when practice is hard, when students struggle at the outer reaches of their ability to learn something intrinsically difficult and stretching. They are set a challenging objective, make a sustained effort to achieve it and are given feedback on their progress so that, once secure, they are ready to move on to the next objective.[4] Along the way mistakes are inevitable – if not, students are probably not pushing themselves hard enough. Such practice should be the meat and drink of classroom life.

From our reflections, we have realised that key to meaningful practice is a ratio: the amount of help the teacher provides during practice and the amount of independent thinking the teacher expects during practice. The ratio will shift along a spectrum from dependency to independence as students become more confident and fluent in new material (as shown in the table below). In some lessons they will be at the 'dependency' stage (i.e. listening to explanations and working with models); in others, they will be working at the 'autonomy' stage (i.e. carefully utilising knowledge and skill while writing a discursive essay or solving maths problems). Sometimes the journey from dependence to autonomy will take a few weeks or even months; at other times the space of minutes. It all depends on the content and the class in front of you. As always, your judgement is most important in deciding when students have had enough practice to move on.

---

4   K. Anders Ericsson, Ralf Th. Krampe and Clemens Tesch-Romer, The Role of Deliberate Practice in the Acquisition of Expert Performance, *Psychological Review* 100(3) (1993): 363–406. Available at: http://graphics8.nytimes.com/images/blogs/freakonomics/pdf/DeliberatePractice%28Psychological Review%29.pdf.

Dependence	Heavy guidance	Light guidance	Independence	Autonomy
Teacher explains and models new content. Students are predominantly listening, watching and taking notes.	Teacher leads practice through questioning, discussion and supports. Cognitive work is shared with the teacher.	Students are doing cognitive work on their own with regular teacher feedback and fewer supports.	Students work with and apply new knowledge for an extended period of time without the teacher's support. All cognitive work has now been passed to the student.	Students fluently manipulate knowledge and skills independently by applying them to new contexts.

Practice continuum

dependence

heavy guidance

light guidance

independence

autonomy

Practice comes in different guises depending on the subject. In PE, it might mean repeatedly serving a tennis ball. In English, it might mean writing a paragraph using three noun phrases. In maths, it might mean factorising a list of equations. In subjects such as science, practice lies in rehearsing, questioning and testing new knowledge. If a child is contemplating a new idea in some way, they are practising it. Often practice will be twofold when we bring literacy into the mix: children practise the knowledge itself and how this knowledge is best represented through oral and written language.

If challenge, modelling and explanation provide the ingredients for learning, practice is the oven in which it is baked. The analogy falls down on one matter however: it is always better to overcook than to undercook practice.

The first four strategies you will read about draw on cognitive science research to consider ways to encourage practice for fluency; the next six consider how you can encourage a culture of deliberate practice in the day-to-day work of your students.

1. The Power of Three

How can practice help students to remember?

In *The Hidden Lives of Learners*, the late educational researcher Graham Nuthall revealed a ground-breaking discovery. To securely learn a new concept, a student must revisit it in its entirety at least three times over a few days or weeks. With his research team, Nuthall was able to record how many times an individual student encountered a concept in class and then predict accurately whether the child would remember it in a year's time.[5]

For example, a student might experience the concept of *chronology* in a history lesson in a number of formats – perhaps through listening to a teacher explanation, then completing a timeline and then writing down a correct definition of the word at the end of the lesson. However, if they have not had at least three exposures to chronology, then the likelihood is that they will forget it. With each iteration, their understanding of the concept might not change significantly, but it is the iteration itself that contributes to long-term retention.

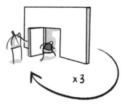

The magnitude of this finding is huge. Most teachers – us included – will, at times, shift the blame for forgetting onto the child: you really should remember this – you only learnt it last week! But when you consider that human memory is predisposed to decay, a fair portion of the burden of responsibility rests on us, the teachers. If we have not provided enough opportunities for students to practise new material, is it any wonder that they have not consolidated it in their long-term memories?

It is not as simple as teaching each new learning point three times over. Nuthall suggests that students learn from exposure to concepts in a myriad of scenarios and contexts – from teacher explanations, to discussions with their peers, to writing an essay. You would be unwise, too, to make the assumption that every child is actively thinking about your

---

5   Nuthall, *The Hidden Lives of Learners*, p. 127.

subject content every moment of your lesson. Your history student learning about chronology may have daydreamed their way through your explanation or spent the whole lesson thinking about how much they need the loo!

Here are a few strategies to consider:

♦ Introduce pivotal concepts and vocabulary at the start of lessons and schemes of work to give students more time and opportunity to practise them later on (see Fold It In on page 139).

♦ Use explanations, models, questions, discussions and writing as opportunities to expose students to key concepts more than once.

♦ Consider lesson plans in terms of how each task in the lesson will enable the child to practise the same material in a slightly different way, deepening their understanding as they go.

♦ Teach less content every lesson to ensure students have the opportunity to rehearse and practise the important ideas.

♦ Use homework as an opportunity to drill and practise key concepts again.

♦ Never assume that just because a student understands the concept once that they have retained it forever.

♦ Bear in mind that wrong ideas and misconceptions are embedded through exactly the same process.

Perhaps the greatest challenge in putting Nuthall's findings into practice comes in the form of fashionable pedagogical approaches that celebrate 'pace' and 'rapid progress' over an appreciation of the enigmatic messiness of learning. Careful iterative teaching is not in vogue, and this may well be standing in the way of the potential for genuine learning in classrooms up and down the land.

2. Mix It Up

How can I plan learning over time so that students are more likely to remember what they have learnt?

Evidence from cognitive science is beginning to reveal the best conditions for learners to encode (or take in) new knowledge so that they remember it in the long term. Two robust findings are important to know about. The first is *spacing*. If we leave considerable time lapses between practising material it is more likely to be remembered. The second is *interleaving*. If we alternate between different problems rather than focusing merely on one, not only is the material more likely to be retained but it will improve a child's chances of success in a future test.[6]

These two findings fly in the face of how curricula and schemes of work are organised in schools. Traditionally they are structured like the left-hand example below, as topic-by-topic massed practice, whereas the research suggests we might be more successful if we switched to the right-hand example, thus activating the beneficial effects of spacing and interleaving through mixed practice.

Massed practice		Mixed practice
Topic 1		Topic 1
		Topic 2
		Topic 3
		Topic 4
		Topic 5

---

6   Brown et al., *Make it Stick.*

Massed practice		Mixed practice
Topic 2		Topic 1
		Topic 2
		Topic 3
		Topic 4
		Topic 5
Topic 3		Topic 1
		Topic 2
		Topic 3
		Topic 4
		Topic 5
Topic 4		Topic 1
		Topic 2
		Topic 3
		Topic 4
		Topic 5
Topic 5		Topic 1
		Topic 2
		Topic 3
		Topic 4
		Topic 5

In maths, for instance, this might mean a half-term is divided into a week each of number, algebra, geometry, probability, statistics and percentages, before returning back to them in a different order later in the term.

However, we would urge caution if you are considering tearing up your curriculum plans to start again. There are hidden dangers afoot. A balance must be struck between teaching for student mastery and teaching for memory; switching from one topic to another too quickly may mean that students do not get the depth of understanding they need in each new topic. For instance, a week of Shakespeare, followed by a week of Greek myths, followed by a week of modern poetry might well provide an obstacle to engagement, which would surely be a mistake. To be told, 'We're coming back to it in six weeks,' at an exciting twist in a story would be frustrating.

Andy likes to think of Mix It Up as a reminder to return to key concepts and ideas regularly in his English lessons, but in an organic and less tightly structured way. When students have been taught what an adverb is, for instance, he insists that they continue to use the terminology in future lessons, all the way to the end of the year. Similarly, there are certain concepts and knowledge that he considers pivotal to the success of his students – such as understanding how to write in an analytical style – and it is these concepts that he continues to refer to in every topic throughout the year.

Another useful application of Mix It Up comes in helping students to plan revision schedules prior to exams. As they are revising, they should be encouraged to avoid studying everything in one block, however tempting it may be. Instead, they should switch regularly between topics and subjects over a reasonable period of time.

You can apply this same principle by mixing up problems during practice. A number of studies have shown that practising a range of different problems alongside one another can aid long-term retention and performance in later tests. This is especially so in maths.[7] Hence, after you have introduced a new concept, set questions not just on your new focus, but mix them with problems from previous lessons. Students must then select the correct method to use. You can apply this tactic to homework too: combine questions on new learning with questions on previous learning. In a similar vein, at the end of each term, design and set a cumulative test. This should cover everything learnt in the year up to that point, rather than just over the past term. Insist that they revise every topic for these tests and give them some lesson time for recap tasks. In doing so, you will be

---

7 Benedict Carey, *How We Learn: The Surprising Truth About When, Where and Why It Happens* [Kindle edn] (London: Macmillan, 2014), loc. 2118–2406.

continually returning to prior learning and activating the spacing effect and interleaving.

3. Build Memory Platforms

What forms of practice aid memory?

A few years ago, still under the spell of the starter/main/plenary model of his teacher training, Andy began to stray. His unimpressive timekeeping meant that he would usually find that the plenary of his previous lesson would become the starter of his next.

Topic 1	Topic 2	Topic 3	Topic 4	Topic 5	Topic 6

Lesson 1	Lesson 2	Lesson 3	Lesson 4	Lesson 5	Lesson 6

Over time, he felt that he had cottoned on to something. This strategy seemed to force students to recollect what they had covered previously, which would then catapult them into the current lesson. When reading a class novel, for instance, he would use a starter quiz to cue memories of past events and ideas. The simple closed questions of the quiz then prompted oral questions – elaboration questions – that encouraged the students to go further. Take the following example.

Initial question: What were George and Lennie wearing in Chapter 1?

Elaboration question: What do we associate denim with, and what might this indicate about the lifestyle of workers like George and Lennie?

The initial question encourages the recall of points of knowledge, like recalling the place names on a map. The elaboration question that follows helps the students to develop this knowledge into a more detailed understanding – the building of roads between the place names, so to speak. The questions also allow Andy to check for misconceptions and learning gaps and to fill these immediately.

Andy's strategy chimes with the evidence shared in Brown et al.'s *Make It Stick*, a book that synthesises cutting-edge studies into memory. The authors recommend spaced retrieval practice in the form of regular short-answer quizzing:

Quizzing provides a reliable measure of what you've learned and what you haven't yet mastered. Moreover quizzing arrests forgetting. Forgetting is human nature, but practice at recalling new learning secures it in memory and helps you recall it in the future.

Periodically practicing new knowledge and skills through self-quizzing strengthens your learning of it and your ability to connect it to prior knowledge.[8]

---

8 Brown et al., *Make it Stick*, p. 203.

They go on to suggest that quizzing is a more powerful tool than rereading notes. Such strategies create illusions of fluency – even though what we read makes sense as we read it, it will slip from our memory very quickly. Indeed, Dunlosky and colleagues, who have reviewed the effectiveness of ten learning techniques, have shown that practice testing is the most effective, whereas rereading is the least effective.[9] Even more interesting is the finding that memory retrieval is most useful at the point of forgetting. The more effort we put into rummaging around our memories, the more fruitful the practice is. Asking students to give reasons why a fact is true – the elaboration question – is also shown by Dunlosky at al. to be a highly effective strategy (it is number three on their list).

Andy now dedicates the first ten minutes of perhaps one lesson a week to a memory task during which each student is compelled to retrieve key information from memory alone. The quizzes work something like this:

Q1–Q3. Retrieve key knowledge from last lesson.

Q4.   Retrieve key knowledge from last week.

Q5.   Retrieve key knowledge from last term.

Q6.   Retrieve key knowledge from last lesson and connect it to knowledge from last term.

The potential permutations of this structure are huge, so what follows is just a possible example:

♦ Which word is missing from this line: 'I sit in the _____ of the wood, my eyes closed'?

♦ What is the hawk from the poem a personification of?

♦ What does the hawk now hold in its foot?

♦ What did the hare in 'Bayonet Charge' symbolise?

---

9   Dunlosky et al., Improving Students' Learning with Effective Learning Techniques.

◆ Which character from *An Inspector Calls* is said to be 'cold' in the opening stage directions?

◆ Which character from *Macbeth* does the hawk most resemble?

Students will undertake the quiz as a 'settler' task. As above, the trick is in asking students to elaborate when they feed-back verbally, so that they switch from surface knowledge to deeper knowledge. The simple questions will often feed-forward into a lively discussion.

The central idea of the 'memory platform' is to ring-fence classroom time for memory retrieval practice. An advantageous side effect of the strategy is that when you regularly plan such tasks, you pay more attention to memory in day-to-day lessons. Andy is much more likely to remind students of previous learning during lessons than he ever was.

The memory platform need not be a quiz, and nor does it have to be used at the start of lessons. The key is to embed regular retrieval practice into the curriculum. A few alternative strategies might be:

◆ Set retrieval practice as homework.

◆ Ask students to test each other verbally: 'A tell B five things you remember about *x*; now B tell A five things you remember about *y*.' This can be supported with cues such as words and images on the board.

◆ Give students time for reflective tasks to review their learning without notes. This could be a page of writing, a concept map or a list of notes.

◆ Encourage students to test themselves and each other, once again without notes.

◆ Educate parents about the value of retrieval practice so that they can assist at home.

In Chapter 1, we mentioned Pam McCulloch, one of the most successful science teachers we have both worked with. At the start of every lesson, Pam would religiously set twenty recap questions. Now, this was not the sole cause, but every year the exam results of her students were nothing short of stunning.

4. Fold It In

How do I build student practice into my teaching in a more organic way?

The question we hear many teachers ask is, 'How can I carve out the time for practice?' Daniel Willingham suggests that one of the ways we might give 'basic skills' the practice they need is to 'fold [this] practice into more advanced skills'.[10] Rather than insisting that children write out the spelling of a new word – say 'photosynthesis' – over and over again, provide opportunities to distribute this practice by applying the word to a number of different written and spoken contexts over time. We would go further and suggest that Fold It In also provides a useful metaphor for how we organise the practice of more challenging ideas and concepts.

The strategy is a useful starting point for planning a scheme or unit of work that takes into account the first three approaches from this chapter – Mix It Up, The Power of Three and Build Memory Platforms. Before planning your next scheme of work, consider the following two questions:

---

10 Willingham, *Why Don't Students Like School?*, p. 125.

1   Which ideas and concepts are absolutely crucial to the overall mastery of the topic?

2   How many opportunities to return to these ideas in different contexts can you include in the plan?

The answers give amazing clarity to planning and lead to some interesting insights:

♦ If an idea or concept is not crucial, then teaching it may take time from the practice of more crucial content.

♦ Planning is better when 'front loaded' so that the difficult content is taught first and then practised later.

♦ Depth is more crucial to learning than breadth. (Consider again the Year 9 science class from the start of this chapter who had been given breadth of knowledge but no opportunity to practise it in depth.)

Here is how Andy has used Fold It In to prepare for a Year 10 Conflict Poetry unit he was planning.

1   He identified the key themes and poetic devices he wanted to explore.

Themes	Devices
The futility/absurdity of war	Patterns of imagery
The fragility of life	The use of symbol and metaphor
The natural order vs. mankind	The sound effects of language
Reality vs. propaganda	The way the poet delivers the final line(s)
The psychological effects of war	The way structural features contribute to a poem's meaning

2   He considered which of the fifteen poems to begin with. He chose 'Bayonet Charge' by Ted Hughes as it covers each of the themes and devices in great detail.

3   For the remainder of the unit, he taught each of the poems through the lens of the ten themes and devices identified. Each new poem provided a new context for 'folded in' practice of each of the ten themes and devices.

4   As the scheme progressed, the students moved along the practice continuum (see page 128), so that by the close of the unit they could tackle a new poem with less guidance.

5   At the end of the unit, students undertook a mock exam to see how well they could manipulate the content they had learnt in extended analytical writing – another opportunity to once again practise the poems, themes and devices.

This structure can be easily imitated in all subjects. A geography teacher could introduce the rudimentary features of third-world urban development before exploring the idea in three very different case studies. A history teacher might consider five concepts – the organisation of society, the role of the peasantry, village life, health and the economy – and return to them in five historical eras. The 'folded in' concepts provide the glue that sticks everything together, and offer a useful conduit through which students move back and forth between ideas and concepts, tacitly practising them as they go.

5. Go Micro

How can we plan practice so that it
leads students towards an overall goal
in manageable steps?

In secondary schools, students usually work towards purposeful goals such as end-of-term pieces of work, tests or
assessments. These help to provide clarity and direction to
our planning as teachers. A common oversight is to devote
excessive practice time to the macro over the micro. To prepare students for future tests and exams, it is tempting to
make them practise with complete past-papers or to answer
whole questions straight away. However, it is often more
useful to first spend time on the small details that contribute
accumulatively to an answer. If not, students can embed
huge misunderstandings into their thinking that then
become difficult to reverse.

A useful analogy can be made with sport. Most professional
sports players practise the micro during training. Footballers
will devote more practice time to micro-parts of the game,
from one-touch passing, to tackling, to carefully orches-
trated set pieces, rather than engage solely in a full-scale
eleven vs. eleven game. Chess players will study the moves
of grandmasters rather than play full game after full game.

Students also benefit from practising micro-details. A good strategy is to give them the chance to refine academic sentence structures in isolation, away from the pressure of constructing full-scale essays and longer exam questions. For instance, students could practise the following sentences:

---

1. *Even though ... , ...*

   (*Even though Curley's wife behaves at times like a cruel temptress, by the end of the novel we realise that she is a victim of a harsh, misogynist world.*)

2. *Some readers might propose that ...; other readers, however, might argue ...*

   (*Some readers might propose that Shakespeare's portrayal of Shylock was cruel and unfair; other readers, however, might argue that Shakespeare was simply reflecting the views of the society in which he lived.*)

3. *The most important word/sentence/idea/chapter/moment is ... because ...*

   (*The most important word from this line is 'top' because it emphasises the superiority of the hawk over its kingdom below.*)[11]

Once sentences like these have been mastered, students can move on to forming complete paragraphs or short answer exam questions, utilising the sentences in longer pieces of work. Once they come to the final extended essay, they will be well-practised in them.

In Chapter 3, we suggested that students model the kitchen sink. They should also practise the kitchen sink. From note-taking to drawing a bar graph, from a volleyball spike to a brushstroke, every fine detail can be enhanced and

---

11 This idea has been adapted from Doug Lemov's blog post: At First Glance: A Sentence Starter Adds Unexpected Rigor to Writing, *Teach Like a Champion* (13 January 2014). Available at: http://teachlikeachampion.com/blog/first-glance-sentence-starter-adds-unexpected-rigor-writing/.

refined by repeated practice under a sharply focused spotlight. This removes extraneous cognitive load – the overloading of working memory – and allows students to narrow their focus. Students tend to appreciate this and can quickly see themselves improving, which in turn boosts morale and effort.

Gradual build-up and repetition of micro-practice makes larger goals seem more achievable. Students move carefully from base-camp to base-camp rather than attempt the full climb in one push. It would be foolhardy for us, however, to recommend that students only practise micro-skills. Exam simulation is important, and it does help with the practise of skills such as time management and coping with pressure. However, it is a fundamental mistake to throw students into the deep end without furnishing them with the expertise needed to swim.

6. Say It First

What role does oral work have in practice?

In the early stages of deliberate practice, students will be making sense of new material. If the work is sufficiently hard, their responses will be tentative and hesitant. The first stage of practice will often be oral through whole-class discussion, Q&A sessions or short paired conversations. The benefits of this over moving straight on to more complex tasks in which knowledge needs to be applied are manifold:

♦ Questioning and class discussion allows you to scaffold and support students' emergent thinking.

♦ Thought and speech are intertwined. Verbalising our thoughts helps to clarify them. Once we find the right words to express our ideas, they are often easier to write down at a later stage.

♦ By listening to what students say, you can pick up on misconceptions much more speedily than waiting to mark a set of books. Your teaching is therefore far more responsive and you can re-explain ideas immediately if necessary.

♦ Consider once again The Power of Three. Verbal practice is an easy-to-manage form of repetition.

♦ Hearing it spoken in formal academic language, by the teacher or another student, helps to scaffold subsequent writing.

A number of our favourite questioning strategies are shared in more detail in Chapter 6. What is most important, however, is that you encourage and guide students towards speaking in formal academic language. The language culture of a classroom really matters and this, we believe, is often more important than any fly-by-night teaching strategy. It is the root, the bone, the beating heart of what we must do.

In a nutshell, this:

Teacher: What does the phrase 'ebbing tide' suggest to us about the poet's opinion of war?

Student: That war goes back and forward.

Teacher: Yes, that war is repetitive and inevitable, like the tide.

Should become this:

Teacher: What does the phrase 'ebbing tide' suggest to us about the poet's opinion of war?

Student 1: That war goes back and forward.

Teacher: Back and forward – how might you rephrase that?

Student 1: It's repetitive like the sea.

Teacher: So war is?

Student 1: Repetitive too.

Teacher: Now as a full sentence. The phrase …

Student 1: The phrase 'ebbing tide' suggests that war is inevitable because the sea never stops.

Teacher: Who can take this insight a little further?

Student 2: War is like nature; we cannot avoid it.

Teacher: Good. Can anyone help her with a better version of 'cannot avoid it'?

Student 3: Inevitable?

Teacher: Okay, fire away in a full sentence.

Student 3: The phrase 'ebbing tide' suggests that war is repetitive and like the tide it is an inevitable part of nature that we cannot avoid.

Teacher: Good. Let's write that sentence up.

The success of this strategy lies in the refusal to accept incomplete or patchy answers, and the insistence that students speak both in formal and subject-specific language. It can feel risky as it involves cutting the pace of lessons. However, the nurturing of this kind of practice culture reaps so many long-term benefits that it should be considered equal in importance to covering lesson content.

7. Make Them Think

How can I ensure that students are encouraged to think hard during practice?

One of the most difficult problems encountered day to day comes from students who write and speak before they think. To consider new knowledge and then put it into written format is not easy. Too often, students race to complete a task, yet that task is an easier one than what we have set. Consider the difference between providing *an* answer to the question and providing *the* answer to the question! Many times, you will see students working hard, but the crucial question is, are they thinking about the topic in the right way? If they are not, then, like Amy in the introduction to this chapter, they might be embedding bad habits or faulty knowledge. Behavioural economist Daniel Kahneman has posited that our thinking mind is comprised of two systems. System 1 is intuitive, responding to sensual cues instinctively. System 2 is slower and more deliberate, and, although often bypassed, it works to hold System 1 in check.[12]

As much as possible, we need our students to make use of System 2 to regulate their own thinking as they are working, so that they think deeply and avoid jumping to swift and inaccurate assumptions, or fall back on bad habits. Providing scaffolds and supports is a great way of doing this. The Education Endowment Foundation, whose research demonstrates the significant positive effects of scaffolding, describe it like this:

'Scaffolding' provides a useful metaphor: a teacher would provide support (scaffolding) when first introducing a pupil to

---

12 Kahneman, *Thinking, Fast and Slow.*

a concept, then remove the scaffolding to ensure that the pupil continues to manage their learning autonomously.[13]

Here are three very simple scaffolding ideas we have discovered and put into practice ourselves.

Slow Writing

This simple strategy is the brainchild of blogger and writer David Didau.[14] When setting a writing task, stipulate not just what you want students to write about, but also the sentence structures they should use. For instance:

Sentence 1: Begin with a preposition.

Sentence 2: Keep to exactly seven words.

Sentence 3: Use a semicolon.

Sentence 4: Begin with a present continuous verb.

And so on …

By making students practise in this way, they have to self-regulate. They are unable to spurt out the first thing that comes to mind. This type of scaffolding is especially useful in English lessons, but it can easily be extended to other subjects assessed through academic writing. Consider the structures – in terms of both grammar and the ordering of ideas – that make up formal writing in your subject area, and work backwards from there. The beauty of this structure is that students have to carefully craft both their language and their thinking – it is impossible to rush. They need to activate System 2 to be successful.

---

13 See: https://educationendowmentfoundation.org.uk/toolkit/toolkit-a-z/ meta-cognitive-and-self-regulation-strategies/.

14 David Didau, Slow Writing: How Slowing Down Can Improve Your Writing, *The Learning Spy* (12 May 2012). Available at: http://www.learningspy.co.uk/ english-gcse/how-to-improve-writing/.

Checklists

Checklists (like the one below) are wonderfully simple ways to embed good habits during practice. As students are working, they tick off the strategies and procedures they have used. It is self-assessment in the moment and, once again, it helps to promote accurate practice.

I have ...	Paragraph 1	Paragraph 2	Paragraph 3
Used a topic sentence			
Clearly identified evidence			
Explored that evidence in detail			
Made a link to the key themes or the context of the novel			

The tick-sheet gives immediate feedback and makes it less likely that a child will pursue the wrong path.

Vocabulary Support

Another very simple but effective scaffolding strategy that Shaun uses day to day in his science lessons is a scaled down version of layered writing from Chapter 1. If students are completing a written task, perhaps responding to a question that requires an extended response, he directs them towards challenging terminology that must be included in the piece.

This is great for ideas and concepts that require the depth of explanation that is often missing when students write extended answers. A common question in science might be: 'Explain how the earth wire and fuse protect a metal toaster and the user.'

This often gets a rather superficial response from students, as many will inevitably produce a fairly safe answer, well within their comfort zone. By providing prompt words to use, they are challenged to answer in more depth. They will now be practising at the outer reaches of their ability.

In this example, the following words should be on display:

Fuse	Wire	Current	High
Hot	Melt	Circuit	Fault
Metal	Live wire	Metal case	Surges
Earth wire	Shock	Person	Safety
Bonus words			
Resistance	Conductor	Plastic	Insulator

The quality of response, from students of all ability, will immediately improve without you having to move around and give too much feedback to individual students. While initially this might be a bit of a struggle, they will feel a much greater sense of achievement when they produce a piece of work with more academic rigour.

This idea can be further developed by asking students for words to add to the word bank not included in the original list. These can then be used by the rest of the class to further redraft their responses. To teach students to write with more cogency, you could also give them a word limit – for instance, 'You must write this in no more than 150 words.' This is a classic example of how scaffolding should not just support students but also stretch them.

Nevertheless, as the Education Endowment Foundation recommends, time must come for the removal of scaffolds. The idea of a scaffold is that it should support a student's journey to a stage of learning they are not quite ready for yet, not be employed as a dependency tool to save them from thinking. At some point you will need to remove the stabilisers and see how they ride alone.

8. Pair Their Writing

How can I get students to practise together?

Paired writing – or any other form of paired task, for that matter – nicely bridges the gap between guided practice and independent practice. Students are independent from the teacher, yet dependent on one another. It is not a substitute to independent work, rather a stage on the journey to independence.

Students work in pairs to produce a piece of writing, perhaps just a paragraph in length (remember Go Micro). The room is usually buzzing with questions: Have you used a full stop here? Why not use a more sophisticated connective? Let's find a better word for … The link between thought processes and writing, so often buried and internalised in the teenage mind, is beautifully exhumed in these discussions.

Here's how Andy organises paired writing:

1 The writing skill to be focused on needs to be modelled and deconstructed (see Chapter 3).

2 The students are given – or, even better, create for themselves – the success criteria they will be working with. This could be made available to all pairs on a simple tick-sheet. Here's an example Andy has used for Year 8 persuasive writing.

Use a discourse marker at the start of every paragraph (excluding the first one).	
Support every opinion with evidence – factual or anecdotal.	
Support every opinion with a second reason.	
Use at least four adverbs to give more emphasis to your points.	
Direct your piece at your audience by using inclusive pronouns.	
Use at least six persuasive devices from the list.	
Use at least one short sentence of less than five words.	

3 Arrange the pairings. There are advantages and disadvantages to working with others of a similar ability or different ability level. Your knowledge of your students will assist you here.

4 Once writing begins, time should be roughly split equally. For half the time, one student is the 'coach', using the tick-sheet – along with a dictionary and a

thesaurus – to verbally support the writer. Halfway through they switch and perform vice versa roles. It works best on a shared, 'neutral' piece of paper. If you like, they can switch writer from sentence to sentence.

It can take time for the pairs to get started but that is part of the beauty of the task. They are thinking, discussing and extending. Or, as we like to see it, they are externalising the internal thought processes that a good writer must go through.

The final written result can sometimes be disjointed and lack fluency; it is not natural to write in pairs. However, you will tend to find that student work is of higher quality in subsequent pieces of independent writing. As we have mentioned, this strategy can be easily extended to other types of task, not just writing: maths problems, for instance. However, we would urge group sizes of not more than two; the more students in the group, the less accountability individuals seem to take.

9. Withhold the Scaffold

When should I withdraw support during practice?

Ultimately, the most important type of practice is independent practice. We recommend that this is undertaken in silence to give students a sustained spell of individual concentration. The opening moments of silent practice are a tricky moment in any classroom. Content and task have been explained, resources are in place, students have successfully negotiated your questions and it is time to let them loose. And then the grumbling begins: 'I don't get it!' 'I can't do this, sir!' 'Can you tell me again?'

The easy option is to respond to these impassioned petitions by racing over to those making the biggest fuss to prevent them from disturbing anyone else. If you give in and placate the student straight away, you are probably communicating three subliminal messages:

1   It is perfectly acceptable not to listen to instructions because you will always bail them out.

2   Effort and thinking are not for every student.

3   Struggle is something to be quickly fixed, not a necessary condition for good learning.

A degree of stubbornness is therefore necessary. The best option we have discovered is to withhold the scaffold for a few minutes – the exact time might depend on the age and proficiency of the class. This might mean refusing to help individuals with a calm but firm, 'I would like you to give it a go yourself first.' It could mean asking the teaching assistant to step back from helping a child for a little bit. It could mean withholding extra differentiated resources, such as writing frames and other scaffolds, just for a while, however tempting it is to hand them out to all who clamour loudly. The unfortunate side effect of making a beeline for the needy student is that it taints expectations: the child eventually will take on the role of 'the needy one', not just in your eyes, but in their own eyes and their peers' eyes too, which then compounds their need and accentuates their difference even further. It is potentially a vicious cycle.

The trick is to plan your differentiated interventions carefully but only put them into action when there is a genuine requirement. In this way, you are responding to genuine needs as they emerge in real time. Our students can surprise us – often wonderfully so – but only if we provide them with the chance to allow this to happen.

You should be warned that this strategy can swing to the other extreme when students become resistant to differentiated intervention, even though the support is probably necessary. A careful balance between tailored support and independent struggle should be sought.

10. Spin the Plates

When should I give individualised support during practice?

No two classes are the same. Streamed or not, every class contains a hugely subtle and complex range of needs. It is also true that no two students are alike in competency. Even if both are working at the same grade or numerical level, their knowledge and skill profile might be very different. One might be deadly accurate at spelling and sentence construction yet lack the ability to explore their ideas in finer detail; another might weave intricate arguments with ease yet struggle with the technical accuracy of their grammar. It goes without saying that knowing your students' strengths and weaknesses counts for more than anything (see Chapter 1).

After you have withheld the scaffold, the time will come when you want to intervene with a student who needs it. Remember, there is a fine balance between healthy struggle and bad practice. As we have suggested before, to avoid having to struggle or in a genuine attempt to complete their work, a student might inadvertently fall into poor habits that reinforce misunderstanding – remember Amy from the beginning of the chapter. So you will need to intervene on occasion, but make sure that you respond to the situation at hand rather than the one you were anticipating. It is important to keep your expectations high so that you do not assume a student is going to fail – if you do, they will catch wind that you do not have faith in them, which will exacerbate the problem.

You can respond in two ways when you spot that intervention is required: individually with the child or collectively with the whole class. A judgement call you will regularly make is to weigh up the cost of interrupting a whole class as they are working. A rule of thumb is that if a third or more of the class seem to be labouring under a particular misconception, practice should probably be halted for all until the problem is satisfactorily addressed.

A useful metaphor for teaching whole-class practice, then, is keeping multiple plates spinning at once – and, fingers crossed, all in the same direction! What follows is a list of simple interventions that you might make at individual or whole-class level while the students are completing a task.

Individual

♦ Highlight a mistake and ask the student to work out the error.

♦ Re-explain a key piece of knowledge they are missing.

- Point the child towards a wall display – perhaps for a sentence stem if they are struggling to start a sentence. Some teachers set up 'stuck stations' for common problems. These are placed in prominent places so that students can be directed towards a scaffold.

- Ask the child to plan their work more carefully before they go back to it.

- Ask the child to reread a sentence.

- Ask the child to start again – especially if the work is messy or rushed.

- Ask the child to read a sentence out loud to see if they can spot the mistake.

- Verbalise the start of a sentence and let the child finish it off.

- Ask the child a question to stretch their thinking.

- Ask the child to think for themselves for another minute – they need to learn the importance of struggle.

- Point the child in the direction of a model to give them further ideas. This could be the work of another student or an anthology of exemplars. Ask the child to go and look at another's work.

- Remember the 'Now try …' trick from the Direct Challenge strategy in Chapter 1.

Whole Class

- Alert the whole class to common mistakes you have spotted.

- Use an iPad or visualiser to present a student's work as a good example and/or to critique.

- Highlight a common misconception or re-explain an area students have struggled to master.

♦ Read aloud a good piece of work.

♦ Ask students to explain how they are struggling and talk through or model possible solutions.

These interventions are just the tip of the iceberg. You will need to combine your familiarity of the children with your knowledge of the subject content. One of the joys of teaching is that responsive differentiation is a game of trial and error, as you seek to adapt with agility to a forever unscripted play. Knowing if, when and how best to intervene is one of the master arts of the classroom. To unlock every stuck child there is a different key, and that key changes not only from subject to subject but also from topic to topic and from day to day.

Reflecting on Practice

What do I do if my students do not enjoy practice?

First, try to work out the cause. If the reason lies in a misalignment between the level of challenge and what the child is reasonably capable of (i.e. the work is too easy or too hard), then this can be rectified by upping or lowering the challenge. If the reason is because the students would prefer 'fun' lessons which sidestep hard thinking, then you will need to dig deep and ride it out. Almost all young people want to do well at school, and once they realise that your high expectations are in their best interests, most will come to respect your insistence on regular practice – if begrudgingly!

Practice can be made more fun through games and the adoption of a broad and rich range of tasks. Drill and kill is not the only option. However, the underlying purpose of practice must remain learning and not engagement for its own sake.

Can intense practice really transform every child's educational prospects?

Despite our enthusiastic endorsement of the growth mindset, we do remain grounded and realistic. Recent research from King's College London has highlighted that a child's genetic make-up is a better predictor of their future academic performance than environmental factors such as school, teachers and family background. The findings make stark reading: on average, 58% of the difference in academic achievement between students can be put down to genetic factors.[15] Infuriatingly, your bright, lazy student will sometimes achieve more than other harder working students. Unfortunately this is a fact of life. The reality that we are only dealt 42% to play with – or less when you subtract the details of family and home life – should not be cause for despair though. All experienced teachers can recount countless examples of students who have achieved remarkably well in the face of major setbacks.

Think of it in another light. If you started to learn the violin from scratch tomorrow, and practised every day for a year, you might not become a virtuoso, but you would be a million times better than you are now. This kind of reasoning reminds us that the right kind of practice can and will make a difference.

---

15 Nicholas G. Shakeshaft, Maciej Trzaskowski, Andrew McMillan, Kaili Rimfeld, Eva Krapohl, Claire M. A. Haworth, Philip S. Dale and Robert Plomin, Strong Genetic Influence on a UK Nationwide Test of Educational Achievement at the End of Compulsory Education at Age 16, *PLoS ONE* 8(12) (2013): e80341. Available at: http://journals.plos.org/plosone/article?id=10.1371/journal.pone.0080341.

Should every student master
everything before they move on?

Ideally, the answer is yes. Pragmatically, it is no. We are working with living, breathing human beings who do not always respond predictably. Practice can never be completely perfect; no student will learn everything we want them to. Indeed, Malcolm Gladwell in his book on the mysteries of success, *Outliers*, has estimated that to achieve expertise in a field, we need approximately 10,000 hours of practice.[16] With the best will in the world, we do not have the curriculum time for this!

Teaching is about striving for the best but sometimes accepting that we will not get there. If we give our students the time and support they need to practise, we are meeting our side of the bargain; however, without reciprocal effort and commitment on their part, excellence and growth are unlikely.

How do I cover all the content I need to and
provide enough time for practice?

This is a tough question. GCSE curricula in England are particularly content driven these days and are becoming even more so. Too often, students have an insecure grasp of a lot, rather than a secure grasp of a little. The Fold It In strategy is useful here. Work out what is most important in your subject first, and then ensure that students practise it to fluency by planning your schemes of work around it. Meyer and Land refer to threshold concepts, 'core concepts that once understood, transform perception of a given

---

16 Malcolm Gladwell, *Outliers: The Story of Success* (London: Penguin, 2008).

subject'.[17] It is these that we must identify, pursue and practise in our subject areas as this is the knowledge that will enable them to gain genuine competence.

Nevertheless, it remains a truism that the reality of curriculum and assessment demands means that all teachers at time face a trade-off between student mastery of a topic and subject coverage. Try not to feel guilty. Packing young people into a building, dividing the building into classrooms and sending them off to study standalone subjects such as English, maths, PE and economics is a modern phenomenon. We call it education – and it is not without its faults. As long as we act in good faith and intend that our students will practise as best they can, we must accept that things will not always be perfect.

If you are really struggling then remember our colleague, Pam McCulloch, and the Memory Platform quizzes. For content-heavy subjects like science, short and regular retrieval practice tasks can genuinely help students to remember larger quantities of information over time.

Should some less able students have access to supports and scaffolds at all times?

Another tricky one. When should you provide support and at what point do you allow students independence? If you release students from your clutches before they are ready, you are tacitly accepting bad or incomplete skills. However, if you give students too much support, they can become over-reliant on it and it can create dependency. There seems to be no easy answer. Flexibility, agility and knowing your students academically are, once again, of paramount

---

importance, which is why Spin the Plates is one of the most important strategies in this book, even if it is almost impossible to master!

Ultimately, this is about raising our expectations of 'low ability' students. When we expect them to struggle, we are likely to keep the supports and scaffolds in for too long. Some might call this mollycoddling.

If students have learnt something well should they stop practising it?

To start with, we need to consider what learning really is. If a lesson has gone well, students will show that they understand the content you have introduced them to. In other words, they will be able to repeat and perform the facts, skills and concepts they have been taught. This, of course, is absolutely essential. But is it learning?

Soderstrom and Bjork make the distinction between learning and performance. Learning must be 'durable' and 'flexible' – that is, it must be usable after the lesson and in new contexts. Performance, however, is 'what can be observed or measured during instruction or training'.[18] Often, what we see in lessons is performance. For instance, by the end of a geography lesson, students might be able to perform by describing the features of a volcano in some detail. However, will they remember this in a week's time, a month's time or a year's time? When they read about a volcanic eruption in the news, will their knowledge of volcanoes help them to understand and interpret this story? If not, then what looked like learning has in fact been a good performance on the day.

---

18 Nicholas C. Soderstrom and Robert A. Bjork, Learning versus Performance, in Dana Dunn (ed.), *Oxford Bibliographies Online: Psychology* (New York: Oxford University Press, 2013). Available at: http://bjorklab.psych.ucla.edu/pubs/Soderstrom_Bjork_Learning_versus_Performance.pdf, p. 2.

The overriding message of this chapter is that the more time and opportunity that is given over to practice, the more robust and transferable long-term learning is likely to be.

Chapter 5
Feedback

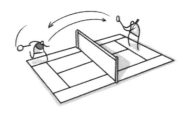

Paul, the English Teacher

Paul is at his wits' end. He teaches a full timetable of lessons and realises the value of meticulous and thorough planning. He is also keenly aware that to help his students become proficient, they must spend a good deal of time deliberately practising their writing. Paul has a young family and a close network of friends, but recently he has been struggling to balance life with work. In fact, he is seriously questioning whether teaching is the career for him.

The cause is a common one: his school's marking policy. Paul is required to mark exercise books every two weeks, give detailed handwritten feedback for all written assessments and engage in a running written dialogue with his students. Paul is drowning in a sea of paperwork. He is caught in a bind. He spends so long marking that he has little time to plan lessons and, seeing as this leaves gaps in students' knowledge, even more feedback is required to fill these gaps. To manage his workload, he has got to the point where he will actively avoid asking the students to write anything down – the less work the students do, the more time Paul can spend with his family.

Things are falling apart for Paul; the centre cannot hold.

James

James is a C student. In every lesson, be it English, maths or Spanish, James seems only to be able to achieve a C. Even when he tries a little harder, James' work moves from a 'middle C' to a 'high C'.

'Not far from a B', his teachers write. 'Keep trying hard and you will get there!' That half-moon of a letter is everywhere: in his exercise books, on exam papers, on reports home and next to his name on the countless spreadsheets that make up modern school data systems.

On GCSE results day, James makes no effort to go into school to collect his results. He already knows how he has done.

Feedback –
What It Is and Why It Matters

Feedback matters. Whether we are trying to find our way to a new friend's house, aiming to improve our performance on the golf course or attempting to learn a foreign language, we need feedback to show us how we are doing. We flounder without it.

When trying to find your way to a famous monument in an unfamiliar city, what do you do? You might start by looking in a guidebook, checking a map or asking a local for directions. After setting off, you will keep your eyes peeled for landmarks along the way and compare these to the map. You might stop to ask someone if you are on the right track which might mean you need to change direction completely. Each of these interactions – with map, local and landmark – is a form of feedback.

As you repeat the route over and over – to and from your hotel – you will require less and less feedback until you can walk there without any guidance at all. Unless you plan to go further afield, of course. Then the cycle will start again. More feedback will be needed to guide you through the next stage of your journey – perhaps to a restaurant in the evening.

The same principles apply to learning. You need to show your students what they need to aim for, set them off and then keep their learning on track through precise and timely feedback, before letting them know that they have got there. Before long, you will be pointing them in the direction of their next goal.

There is plentiful research to highlight the importance of feedback. The Education Endowment Foundation Toolkit, which compares the efficacy of a range of educational interventions, scores feedback very highly – it has a very strong impact on student attainment.[1] This is supported by Hattie's meta-analysis of thousands of studies, which suggests that good feedback can improve the rate of learning in one year by at least 50%.[2]

Seeking feedback is also integral to the growth mindset. If you believe that intelligence is fixed and something you were born with, you are unlikely to ask for feedback on your performance. Indeed, it would seem pointless: I cannot alter my ability, so why bother? Those with a growth mindset take a different approach. They understand that intelligence and performance can be developed and that receiving and acting on feedback plays a key part in this. Therefore, our job in schools is not only to get students to act on feedback, but also to help them realise that the most effective learners actively search out feedback.

Even so, not all feedback is good feedback. Take the example of James, the C student in the scenario above. The feedback

---

1   See: https://educationendowmentfoundation.org.uk/toolkit/toolkit-a-z/feedback/.

2   See the Visible Learning website: http://visible-learning.org/hattie-ranking-influences-effect-sizes-learning-achievement/. Feedback effect size is 0.73.

James received (You are a grade C) was of little use to him. He needed to be shown how to improve. Formative written and verbal comments would have helped, but they would only have been a small part of a larger picture. Feedback should inform James about where to go next, but also inform James' teachers about how to plan for his future progress.

Feedback, at its best, is a reciprocal process. As exemplified in the diagram below, it is not one-way traffic:

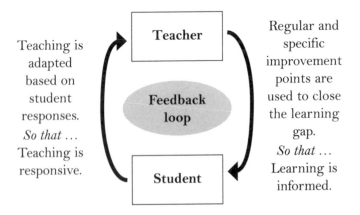

So, the purpose of feedback is fairly straightforward. Following the identification of a 'learning gap' (something a student cannot yet do or does not yet know), the resulting feedback should be aimed at closing this gap. It could be written or verbal, from teachers, peers or even self-generated. The first intention, however, is always the same: to close the gap. Feedback from the performance of the students should then inform your future teaching.

This notion that feedback should inform planning is often overlooked in schools. It might happen in a number of ways:

♦ **In the lesson.** Consider the Spin the Plates strategy from Chapter 4. The feedback you are constantly receiving from students allows you to nip in the bud many mistakes and snags. Stopping, reframing and adapting lessons is an essential feature of good teaching.

- **In-between lessons**. After a lesson, reflect on the inconsistencies, misconceptions and sticking points you noticed. Plan to cover these areas again in future lessons. If you do not, students may never grasp them.

- **In-between units of work**. After a unit of work, reflect on common weaknesses and knowledge gaps. Ensure they are addressed when putting together the following term's unit.

- **When reviewing the curriculum.** Look at performance across certain topics. Where there has been under-achievement or lack of understanding, review how this area has been taught and plan again for next year in light of this.

Hattie and Timperley have identified four categories of feedback generally utilised by teachers.[3] The first is *feedback on the task or product*. Is work correct or incorrect? Are they right or wrong? Such feedback ensures that students build accurate surface knowledge, which is essential if they are going to develop this into deeper learning. For example, in English, have students got a firm knowledge of the plot, events and characters in the novel you are currently reading? If not, it is unlikely they will be able to analyse and interpret the writer's political standpoint.

The second is *feedback based on the process used to create the product*. This is feedback on how students are using their new knowledge. The key to this type of feedback is that it should facilitate error detection and immediate correction. For example:

You need to rephrase that sentence using geographical terminology.

---

3   John Hattie and Helen Timperley, The Power of Feedback, *Review of Educational Research* 77(1) (2007): 81–112. Available at: http://education.qld. gov.au/staff/development/performance/resources/readings/power-feedback. pdf.

Next time you shoot, make sure your head is over the ball to keep it down.

The third is *feedback based on self-regulation.* By self-regulation we mean the way students plan, monitor and evaluate their own work. Essentially, students need feedback on how well they are taking control of their own learning and learning behaviours. For example:

You've worked really hard on using the working-out procedure. This is really going to help you when you move on to more complicated problems.

I can see that you crossed out that first sentence and made it into a clear topic sentence. That is exactly how good writers work, editing as they go. Now have a go with the next paragraph.

The fourth (and least effective) is *feedback aimed at a personal level.* This is based on the child, not the task, and is rarely effective. It will include comments such as, 'You're very intelligent', 'You're great at maths' or 'You're a well-behaved child.' To be effective, praise should focus on the effort and process rather than the child's innate qualities or talents. If not, we run the risk of perpetuating the 'fixed mindset' because a child might interpret, 'You're very intelligent' as 'I have a natural ability at this so I need not put any more effort into it.' Or 'You're not very good at geography' as 'What's the point of trying in geography? I will never get any better.'

The following questions will help you to think carefully about your provision of feedback:

♦ **Does it close the learning gap and/or move the students forward?** If it does neither of these, it is not serving its purpose and so is not worth doing. There is little point in marking a test and telling a child they have scored 67%. Feedback needs to help the child to understand what they got wrong, why they got it wrong and how to get it right next time.

- **Is it manageable?** Our core purpose is to plan and deliver excellent lessons for our students. Anything that stops us achieving this must be stripped away. Feedback strategies must be manageable and sustainable otherwise they will become self-defeating. Remind yourself of Paul, the English teacher from the start of this chapter. The well-meaning marking policy at his school was actively preventing him from teaching effectively. If your feedback strategies are not manageable then they are almost certainly not worth pursuing. In fact, the costs might well outweigh the benefits.

- **Is it fit for purpose?** Different subjects will require different approaches to feedback. What works well in English may not be so effective in maths. Indeed, different types of task within the same subject will require different forms and quantities of feedback. Similarly, some students will require detailed or differentiated feedback whereas others will require only a light touch. As long as it effectively closes the gap and points students to the next stage of learning, teachers need the freedom to make feedback work for them.

- **Does it take the most effective form?** Effective feedback will come in a number of different forms: verbal and written as well as from the teacher, peers and the child herself. The key consideration, then, is not how feedback is given; it is whether students respond to that feedback. Educationalist Dylan Wiliam sums this up succinctly: 'The first fundamental principle of effective classroom feedback is that feedback should be more work for the recipient than the donor.'[4] Precisely.

---

4   Dylan Wiliam, *Embedded Formative Assessment* [Kindle edn] (Bloomington, IN: Solution Tree Press, 2011), loc. 2635.

♦ *Is feedback holding students back?* Even though feedback is integral to learning, too much can be counterproductive. Your aim is to produce confident, self-regulating learners. There is a danger that by constantly directing students on how to improve, they can become too reliant on your feedback and less likely to take risks. Too much feedback means that students never have to struggle, and as discussed earlier, struggle is key to learning. Students must be made to feel that making errors is not just acceptable, but integral to learning.

The feedback strategies we share below have both effectiveness and manageability at their core. Students like James need precise and timely feedback, whereas teachers like Paul need the flexibility to make this workable. Fundamentally, feedback must work for teacher and student alike.

1. Get DIRTy!

How do I get students to respond to my feedback?

Do you recognise this scenario? You have spent the weekend slaving over mountainous piles of books and you have written a veritable essay of red in each one. Each and every student should now know exactly how to improve. You hand back the books and the students race to read their grades, but only one or two read the comments. The rest prepare for today's lesson. And then you ask yourself a question: was there any point in marking in the first place? Nothing has happened as a result of the feedback. Nobody has had the chance to improve.

This is where DIRT (Dedicated Improvement and Reflection Time), a term originally coined by Jackie Beere, comes in.[5] DIRT is incredibly simple but hugely effective. After returning work, a set amount of time is ring-fenced for students to read and respond to your comments. It is as simple as that. They could do this by annotating a first draft, and then completely redrafting using your improvement points as a guide. Equally, DIRT might just be a ten-minute chance to answer a question you have set. Whichever way, students are compelled to make improvements.

The principle of DIRT can be applied through countless strategies. Here are some we find especially useful.

Focused Editing

If DIRT is to be high profile it needs to be built into the curriculum. One approach that could be used across a range of subjects is to get students to respond to the spelling, punctuation and grammar errors which you have identified. We call this Gritty Editing. Insist that students work on their own errors – circled by the teacher – independently, and ensure that dictionaries, thesauruses and any other useful resources are available too.

---

5   Jackie Beere, *The Perfect Ofsted Lesson* (Carmarthen: Crown House Publishing, 2010), pp. 29–30.

Ten minutes of Gritty Editing

1   Correct your circled mistakes. Reread the whole sentence if you are unsure. Use a dictionary to help.

2   Look for and change any mistakes I have not highlighted.

3   If you finish the first three, read the whole piece through again and make three changes of your choice. You can cut out, you can add in.

Rule 1: You must remain silent.

Rule 2: You must not stop working.

Rule 3: You can only ask one question.

A clever variant of this approach to DIRT has been highlighted to us by English teacher and blogger Chris Curtis. As well as changing the mistake, students also have to identify the mistake.[6] So, for instance, if a punctuation error has been circled, the student must, say, add an apostrophe of possession and then write down the mistake in the margin: *missing apostrophe*. This means that students not only change their mistakes, they also have to think about them – a process vital for memory and learning.

---

6   Chris Curtis, Marking – The Circles of Correction, *Learning from My Mistakes: An English Teacher's Blog* (8 March 2015). Available at: http://learningfrommymistakesenglish.blogspot.co.uk/2015/03/marking-circles-of-correction.html.

Individual Improvement Tasks

DIRT is tricky to manage. How can we simultaneously provide thirty students with the personalised guidance they need? Often students will need more advice or scaffolding than a written comment or question is able to provide. One way of solving this problem is to present a slide that links an improvement task to a specific target that you have written in the student's book – shortened to a 'T code' (see also Symbol Marking below).

The example below comes from a DIRT lesson that Andy planned following a Year 9 creative writing task written from the perspective of a Second World War soldier. Students were asked to write a new descriptive paragraph using the following improvement targets:

T1	Try paring adjectives to improve the depth of your writing. *This means putting two adjectives next to each other when describing something e.g. The <u>simple, elegant</u> flower displays its <u>golden, luxuriant</u> petals. <u>Highlight them as you go</u>.*
T2	Use a broader range of vocabulary. *Look up at least five words in the thesaurus. <u>Highlight them as you go</u>.*
T3	Make sure that you use apostrophes accurately. Remember all abbreviations need apostrophes – don't, I'm, it's etc. *Remember to use apostrophes to show possession – 'Dylan's ball'. <u>Highlight them as you go</u>.*

T4	Have a go at using some complex sentences that begin with the words 'despite', 'although', 'even though'. *E.g. 'Despite the cold, I …' <u>Highlight them as you go</u>.*
T5	Make sure full stops and capital letters are accurate. *Be very careful. Check each sentence as you go. Remember that names of people and products must be capitalised. <u>Highlight them as you go</u>.*
T6	Use a range of sentence starts <u>all the time</u> to ensure that you sustain quality writing. *Use the sheet you were given at the start of the last writing task. <u>Highlight them as you go</u>.*
T7	Ensure that spelling is as accurate as possible. *Check every longer word in the dictionary. <u>Highlight them as you go</u>.*

The italicised instructions are the clincher – they gave students the guidance they needed to approach the writing task. Without this scaffolding, it would have been hard for them to know how to improve.

Homework

In a saturated curriculum, and especially in the run-up to summative exams, finding the time for DIRT can be difficult. Setting it as homework is a good option. This works particularly effectively when students have just completed timed exam practice. Set the class their targets and spend a few minutes talking through the general improvement points before setting the homework. Our maths department also use DIRT as part of their homework cycle. A new concept is taught in the lesson, practised for homework and returned to again for a whole lesson of DIRT. The class start by working on general areas of improvement before switching to personal ones.

Log It

Once the DIRT task has been completed, ask students to make a note about how they have improved their understanding. The recording of improvement points can be formalised by the use of a 'progress tracker sticker' or similar document on the front of exercise books (like the one below).

KS4 Allison and Tharby
High School Progress Tracker

Name _____ Subject _____

G F E D C B A A*

Mark your personal target on here. Mark and date each time you achieve a grade on the way.

Date	Improvement strategies

The DIRT process is usefully summarised by the following flow chart:

Focus your marking on a **specific piece/s of work**, that students have had to think about and **produce themselves**. This is more time effective.

During your marking ensure that you:

♦ Say **why an aspect of the work is good** e.g. Good because you have ...

♦ Express **improvement comments as questions** e.g. Could you give an example ... ? How could you explain this ... ? How is this different from ... ?

If students **peer assess work**, ensure it is against clear success criteria. Remind them to ensure their feedback is:

♦ Kind

♦ Specific

♦ Helpful

At the start of the next lesson (when the work is returned) plan for **DIRT** – *Directed Improvement and Reflection Time*. This is dedicated time for students to read and respond to your improvement questions by annotating or redrafting their work.

Students can then do the following:

♦ Completely redraft the piece of work, using the annotations they have made on the first draft.

♦ Make a note of the key points that improved the piece of work for future reference.

If the gap is not closed, a further improvement question may be required

The beauty of DIRT is twofold. It ensures that feedback does what it should: improve student performance. And it redresses the effort imbalance: students work harder on their improvements than you have when marking their books. It's very satisfying!

2. Symbol Marking

What is the quickest way of speeding up my marking?

Instead of writing out comments over and over again, use symbols instead. There are plenty of ways that you can do this efficiently. If you are setting students individual targets, it is likely that many in the class will have an identical target. There is very little point in writing down the same phrase time and time again.

Instead, as you mark use a code on students' work and record the target each time – perhaps on a piece of scrap paper:

T1.　Use a wider range of sentence lengths to help you create the 'voice' of your character.

T2.　Ensure that you begin a new paragraph when a new character speaks.

T3.　And so on.

Each time you come to a student who requires the same target, jot down the 'T number' at the end of their work or next to the mistake itself. Once you have finished marking, simply type the targets onto a slide, present to the students and get them to copy from the slide. It's a great way, once again, of shifting the burden of responsibility for marking away from you and on to the student. The beauty is that you now have these targets saved for the next time you teach this task. Make sure you read them through before you teach the topic again – you can challenge your next class to avoid the mistakes of your previous one. Furthermore, if your colleagues take a similar approach to marking, save time by pooling your target banks.

The approach can be modified for improvement questions too, which often guide students' thinking more precisely than abstract targets. Just replace the T with a Q:

Q1. Why do you think that *The Merchant of Venice* is often considered a 'problem play'?

Q2. How do you think an Elizabethan audience would have responded to this line (in the margin next to the point in question)?

Q3. And so on.

You can also create a code for pointing out student successes. Here is one that Andy has developed:

*** Excellent (about A standard)

** Very good (about B standard)

* Good (about C standard)

! Interpretation of Shakespeare's ideas about racism

£ Close analysis of Shakespeare's use of figurative language

% Knowledge of the way Shakespeare utilises the conventions of comedy

So, if you then write ***! and **£ in an exercise book, the student writes down: 'Excellent interpretation of Shakespeare's ideas about racism' and 'Very good close analysis of Shakespeare's use of figurative language'. Simple.

Code marking has been a revelation to us. Many teachers across a range of subjects at our school have developed creative and ingenious interpretations. Many schools adopt proofreading codes (C for capital letter, P for punctuation, etc.) so that teachers circle mistakes and write the code in the margin. At our school, English teacher Kate Bloomfield insists that students do the cognitive work themselves. When she spots a mistake, she puts an asterisk in the margin so that they have to find the mistake and correct it themselves. We thoroughly recommend that you experiment with symbol marking until you find a way that works for you.

3. Say It

What is the quickest, most effective form of feedback?

Whereas written feedback is very time consuming, verbal feedback is quick, simple and in the moment. In practical subjects, such as PE and drama, it will of course be the only useful form of feedback. In most subject disciplines, even those with a high amount of written output, it will still provide the principal means of giving feedback. It helps you to efficiently steer individuals through the lesson and, used effectively, will ensure that fewer bad habits become entrenched, which will lead to less remedial marking further down the line.

However, there is a lot of confusion in the UK about feedback, with many schools and leadership teams wrongly conflating feedback with marking. Marking is only one form of feedback – an important yet inefficient form. Much high quality, detailed feedback will not require the use of a red pen at all.

Verbal feedback is a far more human process than traditional written marking. Students regularly misunderstand short written comments. What has been dubbed 'dialogic feedback' has become popular in many schools (among senior leaders, not classroom teachers, we should hasten to add): the teacher writes a comment, the student responds, the teacher answers again … This is a little like sending letters via the Royal Mail when you could pick up the phone: all very civilised but hideously slow and inefficient. Through the verbal feedback process, you can check for understanding, rephrase your wording if necessary, fill them in with any missing or insecure knowledge and give them the opportunity to ask questions. It is far easier to be detailed and personalised when feeding back verbally. Look at Chapter 4 and the Spin the Plates strategy for some practical ideas for doing this as students are working.

4. Mark Live

What is the best strategy for giving detailed, individualised feedback?

You can easily formalise the way you give verbal feedback a stage further. As students are working, call them up one by one to your desk and spend a few minutes with them. Discuss their work and then give clear feedback about how to improve and where to go next. You might want to use this strategy to review work over a number of weeks.

This technique works best when a class is undertaking an extended written piece, exam or any other focused individual task. You will be able to see every individual over two lessons and can differentiate the timing of the feedback. Some students need to be left to work independently for longer and others should be steered on track much earlier. This strategy can be manipulated in a variety of ways depending on the subject and task.

Can there be a better form of feedback than sitting with a student, talking about their work and ways in which it can be developed? Even though you will not be able to do this regularly, it should be feasible to see every student once a term. If you factor this in as an alternative to a weekend of marking books, you will have a nice incentive to make it work for you!

Shaun uses this approach in every science lesson. However, instead of calling students to his desk, he goes to them. Each lesson he targets a few students – between eight and ten – and quickly looks at their work for the past few lessons. He then writes a question based on his assessment for the child to respond to there and then. It is a simple but highly effective strategy. It has saved Shaun time and he has seen a noticeable improvement in student work too.

5. Repeat After Me ...

How do I get students to remember verbal feedback?

When giving verbal feedback, especially if you do not use a stamp, there is a real risk that the moment you move away, many will forget everything you have said. Your words of feedback wisdom can become lost in the ether. Do not fear. There is an easy way to avoid this.

After discussing the work, first ask the student to repeat the feedback back to you in their own words. Once you are sure they understand, ask them to tell you the first thing they are going to do. Let them get started and, if possible, return after a few minutes to check they are on course.

By verbalising the feedback and then committing to action, there is a far greater chance that the student will respond successfully. When giving feedback like this, or in fact in any other way, it is important to keep it short and concise. If it is unfocused, the student may struggle to assimilate or act on it.

6. Open a Gallery

How can I make peer assessment work for me?

Peer assessment is a lovely idea: by ceding marking rights to the students not only do they take responsibility for marking, but they also gain a stronger understanding of success criteria through critiquing each other's work. However, it should be approached with caution for two key reasons.

First, a student is always dependent on the ability and commitment of the person they are paired with – if you commit to peer assessment you must accept that some children will give and receive poorer feedback than others. It's unavoidable. Second, students will naturally place more trust in teacher feedback than peer feedback. You are the expert in the room, so why wouldn't they? Remember, you have a stronger subject knowledge and a deeper understanding of the success criteria than your students.

Gallery critique, as introduced to us in Ron Berger's *An Ethic of Excellence*, is a much more attractive option because students receive feedback from a range of others so that the feedback wheat can be separated from the feedback chaff.

The following is an account of how Andy experimented with gallery critique with a top-set Year 11 class and a mixed-ability Year 9 set.

1   In recent lessons, both classes had produced extended writing pieces: the Year 9s a persuasive speech and the Year 11s an answer to an AQA English language question. Before writing the pieces, I gave them a gentle heads-up that their work would be included in a later gallery critique. There was a noticeable sense of care in the work they were producing – everybody likes to impress their peers.

2   The students laid their work out at their tables. Sticky notes were made available on each desk.

3   Before we began, we talked through Berger's feedback mantra: kind, specific, helpful. I gave them sentence stems I had created (see below) to guide their thinking.

Kind

♦ I really like the way you

   _____

♦ Excellent _____ throughout

♦ The most successful thing about this was

   _____

♦ I enjoyed reading this because

   _____

♦ It was especially good when you

   _____

Specific

♦ In the first/second/third paragraph/line ...

♦ I think _____ is quite difficult to understand/
could be explained better/could include more
detail etc.

♦ Your sentence/paragraph/line about
_____ was _____ because

Helpful (refer to success criteria)

♦ Think about adding a

   _____

♦ Think about taking away

   _____

♦ Have you thought about

   _____

♦ To improve your _____ try

   _____

♦ Perhaps you could ...

4   I took an exemplar paragraph from one student's work, photographed it and modelled how to give feedback according to Berger's mantra. We discussed why this kind of well-written, detailed feedback might be more subtle and successful than listing success criteria under the headings 'what went well' and 'even better if'. The Year 9 teacher example is below.

I like the way you use the word 'roam' to describe a criminal – it makes him sound sinister. Perhaps you could change the word 'person' in the second sentence? How could you make him sound more threatening?

---

5   We recapped the success criteria, and I ensured that these were printed out and placed on each desk. I also made sure that every student numbered every line of their work. In this way, they could write comments like, 'Think about adding an emotive adjective to describe the death penalty in line 23.'

6   I insisted on silence for the gallery critique itself. Both classes were extremely cooperative and engaged in reading each other's work – without a peep, in fact. They spent five minutes or so at each table, reading just one piece of work and writing their feedback on sticky notes. At the end of the session, each student had spent time reading five pieces.

7   The final task was to return back to their own work to read the feedback and then to filter it down to the most useful. We discussed how to do this using one or two examples they had noticed during the critique session.

So how successful was it?

♦ The students received more feedback than Andy could ever give them through marking – and in more detail too.

♦ The students seemed intrinsically motivated in both classes. They clearly enjoyed taking part in the whole event, even those who were reticent to start with. There were certainly no loud complaints.

♦ In the best cases, students gave very specific feedback. In the worst cases, it seemed too general – 'sort out your spelling' or 'improve vocabulary' were stock phrases. Nevertheless, it is a strategy that has a lot of traction and Andy is looking to develop it over the coming months.

Classes clearly need to be trained in the language of critique and will need a lot of subsequent practice. You can make the strategy more focused by asking students to zoom in on different success criteria on each separate round of critique – for example: 'First look at the use of spelling and punctuation, and next look at how well they have analysed the historical source.'

Do not forget that students also gain much from reading each other's work. Ask them to 'magpie' the best things they see so that they can assimilate them into their own work when redrafting. A by-product of the process is that students get the chance to read many exemplar pieces. Encourage them to borrow from one another. Insist that this is not copying. In the best classrooms, students learn from each other too.

7. Keep the Peer Clear

How else can I clearly structure peer assessment?

Even though there are dangers in one-to-one peer assessment, if it is managed carefully it can be used to good effect. Our former colleague, David Brading, developed this approach in his geography lessons.

Step 1: Peer Marking Based on Clear Success Criteria

Students are set a writing task, such as 'Describe in detail how humans use fold mountains'. They are then given very specific and clear instructions about how to peer mark the work:

Circle the work when you see any of these. Put a number in the margin to log when they have achieved each of the criteria.

1. *Name of area or country.*

2. *Point about farming or tourism.*

3. *Fact or figure.*

4. *Because …*

5. *This means …*

Step 2: Peer Markers Write Formative Comments

Having marked the work in this way, the marker then has to write a formative comment using the following guidelines:

- ♦ What you did well was …
- ♦ To improve the answer you could …
- ♦ Set them a question to answer.

Step 3: Students Respond to Marking Comments

Once the work is handed back to the owner, their job is to answer the questions set by their marker.

Step 4: Students Log Improvements

Following this, the student transfers the improvement comment to their 'progress tracker sticker' to act as a reference point for later revision.

Peer marking can be successful when broken down like this because the criteria are very concise and instructions clear. Students are not being asked to give an overall grade assessment; instead, they are checking if the work has reached very specific criteria. This means they are thinking about the way that successful components work together. As we highlighted with Open a Gallery, teacher modelling in detail with a student example beforehand can help to ensure that peer assessment like this runs even more smoothly.

8. Network the Critique

How can I use technology to promote a culture of critique?

This type of critiquing works well for students working in a room of networked computers. If, for example, students are producing a piece of work for media studies, they can be instructed to save their work in a common network folder you have set up. You can then access all documents, read them and leave an improvement comment. To save time, these can be copied and pasted from a bank of targets and questions.

At the start of the next lesson, students complete a DIRT task and highlight in green the sections of text where they have improved their work. During the lesson, you can then continue to access their documents, read them, add an improvement comment and then – this is the smart bit! – add a hyperlink to the work of another student whose piece will act as an exemplar. So, you might leave a comment such as, 'Tom, ensure that the colouring of your masthead contrasts sharply with the background of your magazine cover. See Zoe's [insert link] and Amy's [insert link] for some ideas.'

In a sense, you are providing feedback, only this time in the form of bespoke, personalised exemplars. If you do not have access to IT resources like this, do not fear. Maintaining extensive exemplar banks and anthologies of excellent work in your classroom (remember Archive Excellence in Chapter 3) means that you can easily direct students towards useful examples at any time.

Failing that, just ask Tom to go and sit next to Zoe to see her work first hand!

9. Find the Best Bits

Should my feedback only focus on weaknesses and misconceptions?

As well as giving feedback on how to improve, you should also give feedback that clarifies to students what they are doing well. Even more effective is to encourage students to identify and self-verbalise the successful aspects of their work.

When you spot that a student has solved a problem or is producing particularly excellent work, instead of simply complimenting them, try to ask questions such as:

- How did you get to that answer?
- Why did you do it like that?
- Did you use any other unsuccessful methods before coming up with this successful one?
- What was difficult about it?
- What makes it a good answer?
- How is this better than last time (particularly useful during DIRT)?
- What advice would you give to anyone else who is struggling?

Repeating the outcomes of these conversations for the benefit of the whole class will give other students something to aspire towards. A similar approach is to arm each student with a highlighter pen to use as they are working, so when they produce something they are particularly pleased with they can highlight it. This works particularly well with students who have got into poor habits. It helps them to think about what they are doing as they are doing it.

10. Highlighter Action

How can I encourage students to take more care in their work so that they require less feedback on superficial mistakes?

Young people must not become slaves to feedback. We want them to become self-regulating learners, able to review their own work, spot any mistakes and rectify them without the need for us to be constantly telling them to do so. This strategy facilitates this shift.

Equip yourself with a highlighter pen and prowl the classroom as students are working. Disturbing them as little as possible, look for mistakes. When you spot one, say nothing to them, but highlight it and walk away. Do this with a few more students and then stop the class. (Doug Lemov suggests that you simply put a dot in the margin, close to where the improvement is needed.[7])

At this point, reveal to them that any parts of their work that have been highlighted are wrong or need development. (You could vary your highlighter colour here: yellow is plain wrong and green is superficial and needs developing.) Don't tell them why it is wrong or how it needs development – that is up to them to work out. Tell them that they should look at the highlighted parts of their work and correct or improve it. Later on, you can move around the class and check that they have amended their work appropriately.

Over time you should not have to stop them and ask them to review their work – they should just do this as soon as you highlight it. The mere fact that, armed and dangerous with your highlighter pen, you are constantly on the lookout for mistakes should engender more general accuracy in the long run.

Take heed though: you need to get the message right. This approach should never lead to students becoming risk averse in the fear that you will catch them out. Some teachers prefer to use Highlighter Action as an opportunity to celebrate the best in student work. It reframes the emphasis: students are working not to avoid displeasing you but to actively please you.

---

7   See Doug Lemov, Has Anyone Tried a 'Dot Round'?, *Teach Like a Champion* (10 October 2013). Available at: http://teachlikeachampion.com/blog/anyone-tried-dot-round/.

11. End with Struggle

How can I get useful feedback at the end of the lesson to inform my planning of the next lesson?

Plenaries are an odd phenomenon. We have become a little brainwashed into thinking that we should undertake them at the close of every lesson. But do they always achieve what they set out to? The idea is that they are used to 'check learning', yet in reality this is just not possible. Learning involves changes to long-term memory; in contrast, it is fairly easy to remember something during the plenary that you were concentrating on a mere couple of minutes ago!

In reality, many plenaries are little more than a jazzed up version of the following:

Teacher: Well, class, this is what we were meant to be learning today (display PowerPoint slide with learning objectives). *Put your hand up if you have learnt this.*

Class: (Most put hands up to placate teacher.)

Teacher: Great, pack away and stand behind your places.

A pretty worthless exercise! Instead, why not spend the end of the lesson discussing the aspects students struggled with and if they managed to overcome these? Focus time on how they responded to the difficulty.

This strategy has several advantages: it promotes struggle as an acceptable condition, it shares resilience strategies and, most useful of all, it provides you with the feedback you need to plan the next lesson. Take it a stage further by recording these struggles at the end of every lesson for the duration of a topic – perhaps use sticky notes, a whiteboard or a Padlet page. At the end of the topic, you have a ready-made revision list of areas that students have struggled with.

Another variant is to turn this strategy on its head, so students are asked at the start of a lesson or piece of work, 'What difficulties do you anticipate with this?'

12. Five Minute Flick

What do I do if I want to give feedback on written work but have no time to mark it before next lesson?

Before the lesson, check through a cross-section of books (five or six) to assess how students across a range of abilities performed. If they have produced a piece of writing, or any other product, you can begin the next class by selecting an example from one student – typed up or photographed – to critique together.

You can then model the editing process with this one piece, staying focused on the common misconceptions and weaknesses that you identified in your original 'flick'. Point to how this piece both avoids some of these common mistakes and falls foul of others. Once finished, individuals then return to their own work and edit independently with this example in mind.

There are fewer simpler, time-saving and more useful feedback strategies than this. Granted, you have not checked through every book but it is very likely you will have covered most errors. Over time, you can mitigate this problem by showing a wide number of exemplars from a range of students. As with Open a Gallery, it is important that you build up a culture of trust within the class so that students learn to cope with having their work shared publicly. The very knowledge that their work could, at any point, be shared with the whole class is once again, as in Highlighter Action, an incentive to work accurately.

13. Switch the Onus

How do I ensure that students take more responsibility for proofreading, editing and redrafting?

Feedback can backfire. It might seem counterintuitive but conscientious teachers can inadvertently do their students a disservice. Most of us recognise the following scenario:

Jess: Oh please read it, sir. I've tried my hardest. I want to know how to improve.

Teacher: OK, Jess, just quickly.

Perhaps this might be better if:

Jess: Oh please read it, sir. I've tried my hardest. I want to know how to improve.

Teacher: I would like you to reread it, Jess, and make five improvements. When you show me you have done that, I will read your work.

Really, we should take this hard-nosed approach further. Education blogger David Didau suggests that teachers should refuse to mark any piece of work until the student has shown that they have thoroughly proofread and edited it.

Additionally, students should also be compelled to annotate exactly where they would like our feedback before handing in their drafts, perhaps by adding a question mark in the margin.[8]

We have found that many students get caught up in dilemmas about the presentation of their work: I want my work to look neat and tidy, but I want to improve it. Hang-ups about handwriting and tidiness may well have a more damaging effect on learning than you realise.

To account for this, Andy has coined a maxim: Write tidily. Edit messily.

Make sure you explicitly model how to annotate improvements. Some students are unaware that this involves lots of crossing out, adding to sentences, drawing arrows and exploiting numbered asterisks. A great time to model this editing is with a student's piece of work in response to a Five Minute Flick. George Orwell's drafts of *1984* (available on Google) are wonderful examples of the fevered editing that even literary behemoths insist on.

If Orwell had to do it, *so do you!*

You will often find that students' redrafts will generate far more autonomous improvements than your marking could ever do. To avoid the 'writing it up in best' trap (i.e. writing it out again with neater handwriting), always get them to highlight every improvement they make in the redraft.

---

8 David Didau, Getting Feedback Right Part 2: How Do We Provide Clarity?, *The Learning Spy* (5 March 2014). Available at: http://www.learningspy.co.uk/assessment/getting-feedback-right-part-2-provide-clarity/.

Reflective Questions

Can too much feedback create a dependency culture?

Some teachers and schools recommend marking every book, every lesson. Many teachers have perfected quick and simple marking strategies involving colour codes and stickers that make this possible. We would urge caution here. Even though students require regular and timely intervention, too much of a good thing can be counterproductive and, in some cases, can lead to a culture of dependency in which students expect to be spoon-fed.

Students must be given the space to think hard for themselves; they need room to make mistakes, to take the wrong path (see Withhold the Scaffold in Chapter 4). Hold back from giving advice for ten minutes. Insist on individual work. As teachers we must be givers – but we must not give too easily. Doing nothing can often be a better option to doing something. Exactly when to intervene is never clear-cut; it will change depending on situation, student and topic. Once again, there is no substitute for careful, purposeful decision-making coupled with the honesty to adapt your practice when you get it wrong.

What are the dangers of DIRT and redrafting?

In line with our ethos of excellence and growth, we have heartily endorsed DIRT and redrafting. Nevertheless, nothing in education is ever quite as straightforward as it seems. First, in subjects with less contact time (such as RE and music), there is simply not enough room in the curriculum to devote to endless redrafting. Second, we recommend a certain degree of shrewdness when introducing the redrafting process to your class. If you inform students that the opportunity will be there to redraft a piece before they even start the first draft, you may be inadvertently sending a message that 'There is no need to try now, I always have later.'

Second drafts should never be a reprieve for bone idleness. If you are planning to offer later redrafting opportunities, it can be wise not to share this too soon with the class. That way they are more likely to produce stronger first drafts. Alternatively, if a student completes an excellent first draft it may not be necessary for them to redraft. A better option in this case is to present them with a more challenging extension task while the others are redrafting their original pieces.

Is feedback really a 'thing', or is it just part of good practice?

Often the most efficient method of giving feedback is simply to reteach material. Sometimes a class will present so many mistakes and misconceptions about a topic that this is the simplest and quickest method. If everyone is struggling with the same problem, then starting again from scratch is the most obvious solution. A willingness to respond to your own shortfalls is a sign of good teaching. Your class will appreciate you for this. You should never plough on regardless.

Once you know a class well something else becomes apparent. Teaching *is* feedback. You will introduce new content to fit judiciously with what you have learnt about the class. You will circle back to topics they have struggled with so that they can be tackled again from new angles. You will shape explanations, models, practice time and discussion with a finely hewn focus on the strengths and weaknesses of the group.

Indeed, with all the recent hype, you could be forgiven for considering feedback to be the educational equivalent of a wonder drug and a cure for all ills. Sadly, it isn't. In truth, feedback is simply the age-old process of finding out what a child can and cannot do, does and does not know, so that you can adapt your teaching and their learning accordingly.

Chapter 6
Questioning

Anne and Her RE Class

It is Monday morning and Anne is teaching her Year 9s about the Five Pillars of Islam. Most of the class are white British but there are also two Muslim students. Anne explains each of the pillars – the five primary obligations each Muslim must complete in their lifetime – in turn. Her explanations are of a high quality. She uses storytelling and analogy to bring them alive to the class.

Anne looks at her watch and realises that she has been speaking for quite a long time. It is high time that the group got on with today's written task. She asks students to each choose two of the pillars and to write down two things – its meaning and its significance to a Muslim. A number of students get started straight away, but many do not. Very soon Anne is bombarded by a chorus of 'I don't get it'.

Andy and His Approach to Questioning

For many years, Andy's question-and-answer sessions took the same format. He would ask a question, wait for a few hands to rise up and then ask a couple of students to speak. The lessons would go swimmingly. The students who volunteered were mostly of the academic, articulate type. They would say clever things, Andy would nod in appreciation and the lesson would move swiftly on to the next stage.

Yet a problem was brewing. His lessons might have felt fluent and pacey but there were two distinct camps of students growing further and further apart. In the first camp were those who were actively participating in the discussions (along with those of a more introverted nature who, despite remaining quiet, were following carefully). In the second camp were the outsiders: those who chose to opt out of questions and discussions. To Andy, this was fine. They were, in truth, a bit of a nuisance. They would slow down the lesson if he asked any one of them a question.

Questioning –
What It Is And Why It Matters

Questioning is the final pedagogical principle in this book. Although the earlier principles might work well together sequentially – explain/model an idea first, allow students to practise it and then guide them towards success with timely feedback – questioning is harder to pin down. Good questioning is ubiquitous and fluid. It occurs in different forms during each part of a teaching and learning cycle.

For example, earlier in the book we discussed how explanation and modelling can be enhanced by focused questions. In Chapter 4 on practice we also investigated the benefits of regular memory questions. In Chapter 5 on feedback we suggested that writing questions for students to extend their responses is an excellent marking strategy. Even with these examples, however, questioning is such a vital craft to master that it is worthy of its own chapter.

In classical times, the ancient Greek philosopher Socrates tested his students with probing questions; in modern Britain, millions of questions are asked in classrooms across the length and breadth of the country every week. Despite our time-honoured adherence to the humble question, how many teachers ever stop to consider why they are asking a question and what they are hoping to achieve by asking it?

Let us turn to the first of our two scenarios, Anne's lesson on Islam. One of the primary purposes of questioning is *to test understanding of a new concept.* By moving on to the writing task without engaging her students, many were not yet secure in their basic knowledge of the Five Pillars. A combination of knowledge recall questions and open questions (see Move from Closed to Open on page 210) would have allowed Anne to discover how much the students understood, so that she could have adjusted her lesson accordingly. Maybe it was unwise to move straight to the writing task.

Similarly, questioning allows you *to deepen and develop understanding.* Probing, or Socratic questioning (see Probe Them Like Socrates on page 207) is very effective. As a teacher, you should not accept simple or incomplete answers; you should always dig deep for more. You must provoke your students to think. Moreover, good questioning initiates and sustains a high level of academic rigour; the more you probe, the more you push the discussion forward; the less you leave unchallenged, the better your students will learn. A culture of excellence and growth can be created and sustained through this approach. You are communicating to your students, 'In this classroom we always strive for a better answer.'

The second scenario, Andy's question-and-answer routine, brings us to our third purpose. This is *to ensure that students take a share in the cognitive work of the classroom.* Doug Lemov writes about the importance of 'ratio' – the balance of cognitive work shared by students and teachers – during whole-class teaching.[1] Because Andy regularly encouraged students to participate, there was some distribution of the load. However, since some students were given the chance to 'opt out' and not take part, the student portion was not shared out equally. Some students chose to think hard, others did not. The best questioners, therefore, also use questioning sessions strategically to ensure that all students remain attentive and compelled to think, not just the keen.

Lastly, questioning and class discussion help you *to form and maintain your classroom culture.* Do you expect students to answer in subject-specific language? Do you accept incorrect or incomplete answers, or do you expect a high level of correctness? Do you expect them to listen respectfully to each other and to respond sensitively? Do you build and sustain a relationship with your class through this shared medium? You may have noticed that Anne missed a trick in her RE lesson. She should have asked her two Muslim students to share their personal experiences. Questioning a child, even a reticent one, demonstrates to them that you care about their opinion, their life experiences and, most crucially, their education.

Barak Rosenshine's synthesis of research-based principles of instruction has found that the most effective teachers tend to ask more questions than the least effective.[2] Unlike Andy in the second scenario, they also check the responses of as many students as they can, as often as they can.

Questioning also has a philosophical and political intention. Do we want our students to accept the world uncritically and unsceptically? Or do we want students to critique, to contend, to seek compromise and solutions? In our view, an education should teach a child the knowledge they need to thrive in the world, but also that this knowledge is not a

1 Doug Lemov, *Teach Like a Champion: 49 Techniques that Put Students on the Path to College* [Kindle edn] (San Francisco, CA: Jossey-Bass, 2010), loc. 2142–2274.
2 Rosenshine, Principles of Instruction.

stable entity. It should and must be questioned. And so it is imperative that we teach them how to ask questions.

Most of all, questioning is not just a series of simple, inflexible techniques. It should also sow the seeds of rich discussion, described here so beautifully by blogger and one-time geography teacher Andy Day: 'It's clear a teacher is mastering their craft when they hold the reins of lucid discussion that probes, engages, activates, challenges, connects and lifts the centre of gravity of the room amongst the assembled minds.'[3]

In this chapter, then, we will share a range of practical strategies that we, and other teachers, have found useful for creating and maintaining a thriving and lively questioning culture. We will begin by considering how to formulate and manage questions in the classroom, move on to examining dialogue and discussion, before suggesting some ways you can help young people to formulate their own questions.

With time and patience, we hope that you too should be able to 'lift the centre of gravity' of your classroom.

1. Serve and Return

What is the simplest way to ensure that my questioning gets students to think?

As we have proposed, questions should probe student understanding and make them think. A simple way of developing our questioning to support this is by avoiding isolated questions. You should always aim to ask at least one follow-up question to a student response.

---

3   Andy Day, Questioning for Deliberation: TLT14 Session Summary, *Meridianvale* (27 October 2014). Available at: https://meridianvale.wordpress.com/2014/10/27/questioning-for-deliberation-tlt14-session-summary/.

For example, in music:

Teacher: What do we mean by 'texture' in music?

Student: It's the layers of sound we hear in music.

Teacher: That's correct. What might these layers be?

Student: It could be lots of melodies being played over chords.

Teacher: Why do you think texture is important?

Student: It makes the sound more interesting and enables you to create different moods within the music.

This is a really important strategy to focus on. It means that students have to get into the habit of making connections between the new learning and what they already know – a fundamental to learning – and also stresses the point that superficial responses will not be accepted in your classroom. To do this effectively, you need a good understanding of your students so that you can challenge them just the right amount to keep them in the 'struggle zone'.

One of the most effective ways of doing this is to follow up a student response to an initial question with a 'why?' question. For example:

- Why do you think that?
- Why do you think _____ said that?
- Why did you use that method?
- Why do you think somebody might disagree with that?

2. Probe Them Like Socrates

In what ways can I probe a student's response?

Socrates claimed that he was ignorant and had no original ideas of his own. Instead, he devoted his time to asking the people of Athens questions in an attempt to arrive at political and ethical truths. The dialectic method of questioning was used by Socrates to teach the young men of Athens. Through thorough and relentless questioning, they would explore and think through a particular issue, which would eventually lead to a conclusion. Fast forward over 2,000 years and Socratic questioning is still a key component of great teaching.

The overall purpose of Socratic questioning is to challenge the accuracy and completeness of thinking. Six levels of question are considered important:

1   Getting students to clarify their thinking

- Why do you say that?

- What do you already know about that?

- That's a really interesting point – could you explain further?

2   Challenging and probing students about assumptions

- Is this always the case?

- Do you agree or disagree with this?

♦ What is that response based on?

3   Demanding evidence

♦ Why do you say that?

♦ Can you give me an example of that?

♦ Is there reason to doubt this evidence?

♦ How do you know this?

♦ Can you support that statement with evidence?

4   Looking at alternative viewpoints and perspectives

♦ What is the counterargument for …?

♦ Can/Did anyone see this another way?

♦ What are the advantages and disadvantages of this?

♦ An alternative view of this is … What do you think about that?

5   Exploring implications and consequences

♦ But if … happened, what else would result?

♦ How does … affect …?

6   Questioning the question

♦ Why do you think I asked that question?

♦ Have you got any questions about my original question?

♦ Why was that question important?

♦ Which of your questions turned out to be the most useful?

If you are not in the habit of using the questions regularly and think you might forget them, pin them up in highly visible places in your room so that you can refer to them while you are teaching. Don't forget that students can use Socratic questions themselves – give them the stems above and get them to practise using them in group and pair discussions.

3. Move from Closed to Open

Which is more important –
a closed or open question?

The two main types of question are open and closed. A closed question will have a short and definite answer:

♦ Is this an animal or plant cell?

♦ Is Paris in France or Germany?

♦ Was *Of Mice and Men* set in the United States?

An open question is different. It requires a longer answer, which could vary depending on the respondent:

♦ How does a plant cell differ from an animal cell?

♦ Germany has nine neighbouring European countries. What are the advantages and disadvantages of this?

♦ Discuss George's actions at the end of *Of Mice and Men*. How can we justify what he does to Lennie?

In recent times, the trend in teaching has been more favourable towards open questioning. Open questions are of course important. They encourage the respondent to reflect, think and discuss their responses – not only in terms of knowledge, but also opinions and feelings. By encouraging the respondent to really engage with the question they promote dialogue.

However, we would argue that closed questions are just as important. We have already discussed the distinction between surface and deep learning, and the significance of each. Before we move students on to open questions, we need to know if they have got the necessary surface knowledge. This is when closed questions are so important – for checking to see if they know their stuff. If they do not, there is no point in moving on to deeper concepts. A rule of thumb, therefore, is to start with closed questioning to elicit factual knowledge, and then apply this knowledge to questions that require more divergent thinking.

4. Raise the Challenge

How should I plan for challenging question sequences?

It is always beneficial to plan key questions in advance of the lesson. As with the previous strategy, these questions should get progressively more challenging, building from closed to open, each requiring a more complex response than the last. A ladder is a useful metaphor: each question acts as a rung leading towards the core idea or concept. An important part of developing students' understanding is to address common misconceptions head on. Make sure you plan for these too.

So, start with the endpoint. What is the major challenging idea or procedure that you want the students to understand or be able to perform by the close of the questioning sequence?

Here is an example Shaun has used in his teaching. The endpoint, or stem question, was:

> How are enzyme controlled reactions affected by increased temperature?

From this, he began his planning by devising a series of closed questions that allowed him to elicit whether the class's surface knowledge was secure:

♦ What are enzymes made of?

♦ What do they do?

- How do they work?

He then planned some questions to remind them of previous topics they had studied related to enzyme controlled reactions:

- What does increasing the temperature do to the motion of molecules?

- What does increasing the temperature do to the rate of chemical reactions?

Such questions help students to recall prior knowledge and make links across topics. Finally, he planned a series of questions that linked these ideas together to develop more conceptual learning:

- What will the increased temperature do to the motion of the enzyme molecules and substrate molecules?

- What will be the result of this?

- If the temperature is increased further what will happen to the molecules that make up the enzyme active site? What will this do to the shape of the active site? What will this do to how well the enzyme works?

A common misconception Shaun has encountered is that enzymes 'die' – the belief heat kills them and causes them to stop working. Enzymes, of course, cannot die: they are molecules, not living organisms. Heat denatures them (changes their molecular structure) and so stops them from working. With this in mind, Shaun also planned some questions to address these misconceptions:

- Once the enzymes have stopped working, is it correct to say that they have died?

- Why is this not a correct statement?

- What is the correct explanation for this?

The reason for staging your questioning in this fashion is that all students can get on the ladder at any point. If you do not start with the key knowledge bottom rungs, some will quickly lose track. Your questions should aim to support all to the top – to a solid understanding of the original stem question. It may seem that planning questions with such rigour is laboriously time consuming, yet it is a highly effective approach that should not be dismissed.

5. Respond in the Moment

How can I prepare for the fact I can never know exactly how students will respond to my questions?

Classrooms and student responses are highly complex. If we want our questioning to be personalised, supportive and probing, it can be hard to see how you can plan every question. Of course, stem questions and other key questions can be planned in advance, but as soon as students start responding, the script often has to go out of the window. Lessons are never carefully scripted and rehearsed stage productions, even though sometimes you probably wish they were! Instead, you will need to think on your feet and shape your questions around the answers in real time, as they pop up in all their unexpected glory.

The following example of a short questioning sequence demonstrates both student responses and the kind of sharp thinking required by the teacher:

Teacher: So, what do you think Curley's wife's role in the novel is? You have twenty seconds to think about it …

(Pause.)

Teacher: Josh, what do you think?

(My question was deliberately vague; I am after divergent thinking here. I pick Josh for a reason – like some others in the class, he jumps to conclusions too quickly. This is my chance to challenge these preconceptions from the off.)

Josh: I think she is meant to be the evil character because she destroys the dream.

Teacher: When do we see her behave like this?

Josh: Well, when we first see her she cuts off the light in the doorway.

Teacher: Is that enough to call her 'evil'?

Josh: No, not really. She also treats Crooks badly and flirts with Lennie which leads to him killing her.

Teacher: Interesting. Matt do you agree with Josh?

(I have probed Josh to give evidence, yet remained non-committal about his response. Matt's thinking is more refined and I know he will challenge Josh.)

Matt: To an extent, but the way Steinbeck describes her death makes her seem weak and defenceless.

Teacher: Do you remember how Steinbeck described her?

Matt: No, not quite.

(Emily's hand goes up. I nod to her. If I did not allow hands-up at times this useful addition would not have occurred.)

Emily: She was 'very sweet and young'.

(I look back at Matt. He is used to my body language. He knows I expect him to say more.)

Matt: So 'young' shows … (I shake my head; 'shows' is a banned word) *illustrates that she is just an innocent child.*

Teacher: Right everyone. Josh suggests that Curley's wife is evil, yet Matt feels she is innocent. Have a think about it. Where do you stand?

(Pause. Choose Sian.)

Sian: Well, I think she has some of the characteristics of a villain but she's also a victim. Steinbeck was making a comment about women in those times: Curley's wife is a victim of a masculine society who has no choice but to be the villain.

Teacher: A* answer, Sian. Wow. That's the kind of balanced interpretation we're looking for everyone.

(Because, for me, class discussion is about searching together for the best ideas, I think it is important to stop and draw attention to quality answers. If praise is overused, I find it can put a stopper on the discussion; you can inadvertently send out the message that that was good enough, no more need be said.)

Teacher: So, Sian, are you sure there were no other choices available to her?

(All assumptions, even the best, can be challenged.)

All in all, the best questioning combines intricate planning with the best of improvisation. For us, this is why classroom teaching is such an exciting yet challenging job.

6. Rouse the Dead

What do I do about 'I don't know'?

There will be times when, despite your best questioning efforts, a child will respond with 'I don't know' or sometimes even with a desultory shrug of the shoulders. In these moments it can be very tempting to pass the baton over to another student who is champing at the bit to answer. But doing so would be a grave mistake. If you let a child off the hook too easily, you are subtly communicating the message that you have little faith in their ability to answer the question – and children do pick up on these cues.

Thankfully, there are plenty of sleights of hand that allow you to guide your students towards success in this scenario. Each of the following examples can be used as initial questions or rephrased ones.

♦ Give the student the answer you are looking for and ask them to explain how you got there:

> *Teacher: Which word in that sentence is the adjective?*
>
> *Student: I don't know.*
>
> *Teacher: The answer is 'uncompromising'. Why is that the right answer?*
>
> *Student: Because an adjective describes a noun and 'uncompromising' is describing 'the man'.*

♦ Give them two options and get them to explain which they agree with most:

> *Teacher: Give me a word that best describes the inspector in this scene.*
>
> *Student: I don't know.*
>
> *Teacher: Is he 'impressive' or 'cowardly'?*
>
> *Student: He is impressive because he does not back down to the pressure Mr Birling attempts to put on him.*

♦ Remind them of the facts:

> *Teacher: Do you think that J. B. Priestley had an optimistic or pessimistic view of the older generation?*
>
> *Student: I don't know.*

> *Teacher: OK, remember that Eric and Sheila are both ashamed of their actions whereas Mr and Mrs Birling refuse to take responsibility for their own.*
>
> *Student: I think he is pessimistic about the old because they stick to their guns and refuse to change.*

♦ Rephrase as a comparison:

> *Teacher: What is a cubed number?*
>
> *Student: I don't know.*
>
> *Teacher: What is the difference between a cubed number and a squared number?*
>
> *Student: Oh, a squared number is when you times it by itself. A cubed is when you times it by itself twice.*

♦ Think, pair, share:

This well-known manoeuvre is particularly useful when the whole class are unforthcoming. Ask them to think about the question individually (and perhaps jot down one or two notes), discuss it quickly in pairs and then ask them for their answers. Make students individually accountable by informing them that you will randomly select a few students to respond.

If these are not successful, Doug Lemov highlights a further approach: no opt out. Here, you ask another student for the answer and then come back to the original student, asking them to repeat this answer.[4]

Don't forget, there is often a good reason why a child is unable to answer a question. This might be for a myriad of reasons. One of the purposes of asking questions is to find out how much the students know, but when it is clear that a

---

4   Lemov, *Teach Like a Champion*, loc. 837.

number are struggling then you will need to address the surface knowledge first.

Don't forget there might be a myriad of reasons why a child is unable to answer a question. Let's say you are an English teacher asking a class to interpret a writer's attitude on a particular theme. You can turn the tables by taking on the role of the writer and asking the class to devise questions for you in role. Or if you are teaching a class about electrons, why not become a talking electron yourself! It is a simple, fun and unthreatening way to fill in the gaps in knowledge and understanding that are standing in the way.

The final option is to simply stop the questioning and teach. It can be frustrating when the discussion has not elicited the level of perception you are after, but this is entirely normal. As the expert in the classroom, you will often need to make the call to stop and re-explain the learning they have yet to fully grasp.

7. Support the Struggle

How do I ensure that I do not accept superficial answers from students?

This strategy builds on those above. It is vital that we do not accept superficial or underdeveloped answers. We need to set the standard, and this standard should be rooted in academic language and thought. Our questioning should scaffold a student's thinking, providing the support needed to answer tough and intellectually demanding questions.

Imagine you were to ask the question: why does a marble falling through water reach a terminal velocity? You may well need to break down the question into multiple stages to guide the students' thinking:

Teacher: OK, so what are the two forces acting on the marble?

Student: Gravity and upthrust?

Teacher: Correct. Initially, which force would be greatest?

Student: Gravity.

Teacher: Yes, how would the marble be moving?

Student: Accelerating.

Teacher: Great. As its speed is increasing, what would happen to the size of the upthrust force?

Student: It would increase and eventually be the same size as the gravitational force.

Teacher: Exactly, so what would this mean about the motion of the marble?

Student: It would move at a constant speed.

By putting one student in the spotlight like this, your questioning models the causal thinking required to understand an idea logically. This approach supports them through the 'struggle zone' and, with a bit of luck, they are developing resilience in your subject: science is hard, but if I keep trying I know I can get there. Over time you will find that you have set an expectation, and students will habitually extend their answers with less need for prompts. When they stop too soon and do not fully develop an idea, a simple cue (such as an inquisitive raise of the eyebrows) is often enough to get them to explain themselves more fully.

8. Remember to Pause

How else can I ensure that students' responses are likely to be detailed and considered?

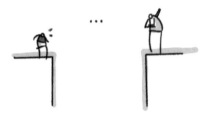

Too often we ask questions and expect students to answer immediately. If we do not give 'wait time', we are not giving students the space to cognitively process a thoughtful response. Thinking deeply takes time and effort – and a good deal of patience on your part too.

Pausing can operate on a number of levels. Very simply, after asking a question, wait for three to five seconds and then ask for responses. Resist the temptation to break the silence. This is difficult and will feel unnatural – which is why many teachers cannot sustain it. However, because the students have had time to think deeply, it often results in a fuller, richer response.

For more challenging questions, allow for an even longer wait time – twenty to thirty seconds, perhaps. Andy finds it useful to narrate over the silence in a soft, non-intrusive voice:

I'm going to give you twenty seconds to think about this question ... Now, you should now be rehearsing in your mind what you will say if I ask you ... Five, four, three, two, one ... Natalie, I'd like you to lead off.

Think, pair, share (see Rouse the Dead on page 215) is another useful way to introduce wait time. Furthermore, research indicates that pauses of two or three seconds are also beneficial after the student has finished speaking and before the teacher interjects to evaluate the response. It seems to give the student time to expand and reflect on their answer, or even in some cases, to backtrack, modify and further elaborate on their answer.[5]

9. Involve Everyone

How do I encourage all students to listen to, think about and respond to my questions?

When asking questions there are a number of ways in which students can be expected to respond. There is much disagreement about the right approach, but arguably the best approach is to use a purposeful combination of them all to fit the situation.

Hands-Up

Hands-up is the traditional approach. You ask the question and then hands shoot up from those who either think they know the answer or who like to revel in the limelight. An argument against this approach is that only the keen or extrovert students put their hands up, leaving the others safe in the knowledge that they will not be expected to answer or contribute. Cast your mind back to the mistakes Andy was making in the scenario we shared at the beginning of this chapter.

---

5   Wiliam, *Embedded Formative Assessment*, loc. 1741.

Nevertheless, with a little finesse there are still some strong advantages to this approach. A simple hands-up can provide you with rich data about who knows what in a split second. If you have just taught a fundamental concept and you want to know if the class understands it before you move on and develop the idea more deeply, you could ask a subtle question like, 'Who would feel confident to answer the question, "What are the factors required for photosynthesis"?' If nobody raises their hand, there is little point in moving on to the next topic, which might be how leaves are adapted for photosynthesis.

If only a few raise their hands, select somebody who has kept theirs down and ask them what they are struggling with. This way, keeping your hand down no longer becomes a means of opting out of the discussion. If lots of students put their hands up, you need to check that they genuinely know and they are not just placating you! At this point, use Socratic questions to probe their understanding.

A further variation is to ask students to put their hands up if they don't understand a question. Once again, there is no way of opting out. If you leave your hand down you will also be expected to answer.

Random Questions

Random questions can be organised in a number of ways. Computerised random name generators are available, but the common approach is to use lolly sticks labelled with student names (or with the numbers 1–30 relating to place on the register). A stick is picked at random to determine who will answer. The advantage of this method is that, yet again, there is no option to disengage – all students have to be prepared to answer in case their name is selected. A second benefit is that, as a teacher, there is no option to subconsciously exclude any member of the class.

The best approach is to plan for progression and implement it like this:

- Ask your question – for example, 'What are the two chemicals required for aerobic respiration?'

- Then pause while you pick the name.

- If it is a lower-ability student, see whether they can answer the question first off. If not, scaffold the question for them by breaking it down into smaller questions or by using some of the tricks we included in Rouse the Dead (on page 215).

- If the student can answer straight off, make sure they give you a detailed and well-rounded response and then ask them a follow-up question.

Directed Questioning

Directed questioning is when you choose who you are going to ask. Doug Lemov calls this 'cold calling'.[6] During the lesson you will have a good understanding about who has been following the learning and who has been struggling. You may already have put in place a variety of strategies to support the struggling students, so it would be perfectly sensible for you to direct a question at one of them. Alternatively, over a series of lessons, you might need to target certain students – perhaps you want to boost their confidence or give them more incentive to stay focused and attentive.

Doug Lemov's work has also highlighted a subtle shift you can make to your questions.[7] Often, teachers will phrase a directed question like this:

---

6 Lemov, *Teach Like a Champion*, loc. 2528.
7 Lemov, *Teach Like a Champion*, loc. 2703–2728.

John, can you give me three factors that contributed to the outbreak of the First World War?

By saying 'John' at the start of the question, you are immediately letting the rest of the class off the hook. They know they will not be required to respond and so there is no compulsion to think through an answer for themselves. Instead, rephrase the question like this:

I'm looking for three factors that contributed to the outbreak of the First World War ... (pause) ... John?

This is a small but vital tweak. Used regularly over the academic year, you will dramatically increase the quantity of thought that takes place in your lessons.

Hybrid Option

A final approach is the hybrid option. Randomly generate or cold call to begin with, and then when this dries up, hear from those who have their hands up. This way, students who have questions to ask or can move the discussion forward can be heard from, yet they do not dominate the lesson. This is Andy's daily approach to questioning.

10. Chain the Questions

How can I encourage students to listen and respond to one another?

Think back to Support the Struggle, when you broke down questions to scaffold student answers. One way of encouraging children to keep on their toes and stay with a discussion is to share the questions across the class:

Teacher: OK, so what are the two forces acting on the marble … Karen?

Karen: Gravity and upthrust.

Teacher: Correct. Initially, which force would be greatest … Tom?

Tom: Gravity.

Teacher: Yes, how would the marble be moving … Ayasha?

Ayasha: Accelerating.

This approach encourages careful listening and keeps each member of the class attentive – it could be them next. This kind of quick-fire questioning is excellent for revision lessons and recap tasks, especially when you are looking for factual answers.

You can upgrade chained questions too. Whoever answers your question must think of another related question to ask somebody else. This idea can be developed in a number of ways. Instead of just giving students the freedom to come up with their own question, have a few sentence stem words on the board (e.g. Why? What? How? When? Where?). Indicate which word the student's question must start with. This allows you to vary the type of questions that are asked.

A further alternative is to create a 'why chain'. For every answer given, ask a new 'why?' question to be answered by the next person:

Q. Why do we need laws?

A. To control people.

Q. Why does society need to control people?

A. Otherwise it would lead to chaos.

Q. Why would it lead chaos?

---

11. Probe the Continuum

How can I use open questions to promote enquiry and discussion?

What follows is one of the simplest yet most effective strategies for generating classroom discussion we have come across. It works best for open questions that encourage a wide spectrum of responses.

Choose a question – for instance, 'Did the writer present a completely pessimistic view of the world in this novel?' Then show a continuum from 'yes' to 'no' on the board:

Give each student a sticky note on which to write their name and tell them that they can stick the note on the continuum wherever they like. As you hand them out, let students chat to their neighbours about where they will place their sticky notes. You can feed in a few ideas to those who are unsure or lack confidence as you go round.

Once all the sticky notes are up the discussion ensues. You will now know the broad sweep of opinion in the class and can conduct the discussion however you like. You might use the *Countdown* approach: pick 'one from the top', 'one from the bottom' and 'one from the middle'. As you pick off the sticky notes, ask students either to comment on the reasoning behind their position or challenge an opposing viewpoint. As always, it is important to probe and to refuse to accept insufficient or poorly reasoned points. Give students the option to move the note to a different position along the continuum mid-discussion.

The idea can be developed in a number of ways. For example, you could add some key words or phrases below the continuum line that students could be encouraged to use in their responses. If you want to encourage students to develop or question an idea or opinion that one of their peers has offered, assign a 'challenge', a specific hand gesture (such as a thumbs-up) so you can select students to speak from the floor as well as from the board.

So why does it work? First, unlike some other 'no opt-out' strategies, there is lots of opportunity to think ideas through before speaking. Second, the continuum promotes balanced, shades of grey thinking. Third, if used judicially in the learning cycle it can feed directly into the scaffolding of writing.

Two words of warning before you give this a try. Be careful when wording the question that you do not give students an option to take up a weak line of argument that could lead to genuine misconceptions. Note how the question above asks the question, 'Did the writer present a *completely* pessimistic view of the world in this novel?' rather than, 'Did the writer present a pessimistic view of the world in this novel?' Watch out, too, for those shrinking violets who try to hide their sticky notes under another's!

12. Orchestrate the Discussion

How can I conduct rich and focused discussions and debates?

The effective questioner will use a range of questioning strategies to facilitate the flow of classroom discussion and to avoid a series of unconnected, atomised student responses. In the first instance, you should practise some stock phrases to provide this all-important linkage:

That links really closely to what Sarah just said – Sarah can you just repeat your last comment?

Tom, I really like the way you have given a reason to back up your argument. Does anyone else have another reason they could add to support his argument further?

So Lindsay agrees with the protestors that we just read about in the text. John, I know from the discussion you and Tom were having earlier that you disagree. Can you share your reasons with us please?

Zoe, thanks for reading out your response to that question. Tim, what impressed you particularly about Zoe's answer?

Hold on to that thought, John. I'll be coming back to you shortly.

So John thinks the idea is wrong, yet Hassan thinks it's right. Brian, is there a third option?

Your role here is to weave the web of the discussion and to gently define the differing shades of thought, so that the class probe the topic with sensitive attention to detail. Your ultimate aim, however, should be to encourage students to make the connections between comments themselves. The truth behind the most disciplined discussions is that students listen to and respond to each other with little interruption from the teacher.

One simple way of doing this is through ABC feedback – Agree with, Build on or Challenge. After you have heard one idea, ask the next student whether they would like to ABC. Insist that they comment on the previous student's remark and that they speak formally: 'I would like to build on Adam's comment ...'

Some students will take this to a new level: 'I partly agree with Adam's point that ... However, I would like to challenge his point about ...'[8]

Finally, class, group and paired discussions can also be scaffolded through the use of discussion stems. Make these highly visible in your room and insist students use them until they become habitual. Here are a few possibilities:

♦ I agree with _____ because _____.

♦ After listening to what _____ said, I think _____.

♦ I think we also need to consider _____.

♦ Similarly to _____ I think _____. However, I also think _____.

♦ I see it differently to _____ because _____.

♦ I'd like to ask a question: _____?

Think carefully about the stems you choose: make sure they are sharply focused on the academic register appropriate for your subject. While it is tempting to pin twenty or thirty stems up around your room, it is advisable to filter them to five or six as we have here. With practice, students are much more likely to perfect a smaller number. Insisting that students use each other's first names, as you may have noticed

---

8   This idea originally came from Alex Quigley's blog post, 'Disciplined Discussion' – As Easy as ABC, *Hunting English* (26 December 2013). Available at: http://www.huntingenglish.com/2013/12/26/disciplined-discussion-easy-abc/.

in the examples, helps to inspire a respectful, conscientious and listening atmosphere.

13. Use Hinge Questions

How can I use diagnostic questions to gain a clear picture of where students are and where I need to take the lesson?

A hinge question is a popular way of checking the understanding of all students at a key point in a lesson before moving the learning on. Again, they are useful in terms of judging whether students are at the right point to move on to more challenging work, or whether they need more time to master what they are currently working on. A good hinge question should:

♦ Be quick and easy for the teacher to ask.

♦ Be quick for the students to respond to – multiple choice questions are a popular option.

♦ Be designed so that a student is only likely to get the answer right if they understand the key point.

♦ Be designed so that wrong responses inform the teacher about the misconceptions the student may have.

Consider the following example. Your science students have been learning about heat transfer by convection. You want to check that they have understood this key concept before going on to teach how it influences other processes – on-shore breezes and so on. You show them a photo of a hot air balloon and pose the following hinge question with four possible answers:

The hot air balloon moves upwards because:

A. Heat rises.

B. Hot air is lighter than cold air and so floats upwards.

C. Hot air is less dense than cold air and so floats upwards.

D. Hot air particles are lighter than cold air particles and so lift the balloon upwards.

If they have understood convection they would know that C is correct. This is a good hinge question because it is quick and easy to ask, all students can respond at the same time (they could use laminated ABCD cards or mini-whiteboards) and it carefully targets the concept of convection. The other responses highlight common misconceptions, so if many students have picked these there would be no point in moving the lesson on until these have been addressed. A student picking response D, for instance, might be harbouring a misconception about the particle theory of matter. Air particles have the same mass, irrespective of whether they are warm or cold; it is their movement, and therefore their density, that is affected by temperature.

A note of caution, however, about using ABCD cards or mini-whiteboards in this way. If students hold them up as they please, those lacking in confidence may try to follow the lead of others. A much better alternative is to ask students to select their answer, countdown from three and expect everyone to reveal their answer simultaneously.

Are formative assessment techniques like hinge questions evidence of genuine learning? No, not exactly. Do they suggest to the teacher that students have understood the idea at that time and are able to recall it there and then? Yes, most likely. Cast your mind back to Chapter 4: before an idea becomes secure in a child's long-term memory, they are likely to need repeated exposure to it. Never assume that just because students understand the concept now that they will remember it indefinitely.

14. Devise the Questions Themselves

How can I support students to ask questions themselves?

If you want your students to gain independence, to become owners of their own learning, you will need to encourage them to ask their own questions. The more you know and understand, the more curious you are to find out more – and when we are curious, we ask questions. When students ask questions they are more likely to discover gaps in their own understanding and work out what they need to do or find out next.

A useful approach is to find ways of scaffolding students' questions. The Question Generator makes use of common 'command words' (e.g. identify, describe, explain) along with other frequently used terms. The example below is particularly useful for the sciences. You may need to devise your own to fit your subject discipline. (A good way to find the key terms in your subject is to leaf through past exam papers identifying commonly used terminology.) Students might use this generator to come up with questions for their peers during the lesson or to create questions that they would like answered.

The Question Generator

				Happen
Identify	Why	Is		Change
Describe	How	Did		Cause
Explain	When	Can		Result
Analyse	Where	Would		Affect
Compare	What	Will		Find
Evaluate	Who	Might		Same
Justify				Different
				Advantage
				Disadvantage
				Improve
				Agree
				Disagree
Use one word from all or some of the columns to come up with some great questions.				Strength
				Weakness

- **Science:** Can you *describe why* some people might *disagree* with a limestone quarry being built near to their house?

- **Religious education:** Can you *explain how* somebody who believes in absolute morality *might* respond to the commandment 'do not kill'?

- **Geography:** Can you *describe how* humans using resources from a tropical rainforest *might result* in problems for animals living in the rainforest?

These questions could be used in a variety of ways: as written tasks for classwork, homework or revision; to be parked and then returned to later in the topic; or simply as questions to ask the teacher in a reverse Q&A session.

Another time to encourage students to ask questions is at the beginning of a new scheme of learning to ignite student curiosity. This is similar to the Open the Gap strategy in Chapter 2. An unusual or mysterious visual or physical 'hook' – like a picture or an object brought into the room – can act as a stimulus and foster the desire to know more.

In science, even though students might understand how and why a patient requires dialysis, they might not have considered the impact it has on a patient's day-to-day life. A photo of a patient receiving dialysis can kindle a variety of questions: how long do they have to stay connected to the machine for? What does the machine actually do? What would happen to the patient if the machine was removed or failed?

In PE, students could be shown images of sponsorship in sport. They could come up with a range of questions regarding sponsorship, which could then be chiselled down into one killer question. Perhaps this could be the hook for a class discussion or the starting point for a modelled extended written answer: what are the advantages and disadvantages of sponsorship for the sponsor, the performer and the sport/event?

Reflecting on Questioning

What are the common mistakes teachers make when asking questions?

There are many, but here are a few mistakes we have both made – and learnt from.

- **Getting students to guess.** This often happens with new vocabulary. 'Who can tell me what the word "myopic" means?' This may lead to much guessing as you desperately try to provide clues as if you were playing a game of charades – such as pointing to your eyes or gift-wrapping the answer with the clue 'It's the opposite to long sighted.' In maths, it might be, 'Who can tell me the formula for speed?' when you have yet to teach it. It is a waste of time; you are better off telling the class rather than asking them to guess what you are thinking.

- **Asking the wrong student at the wrong time.** Be mindful of who you are asking. If you know that the student does not have any hope of answering the question, you are better off leaving the child for the time being or rephrasing or simplifying the question. Look at some of the techniques we shared in Rouse the Dead (on page 215) to help with the rephrasing.

- **Asking an open question before teaching the knowledge needed to answer it.** Imagine if you were to start your scheme of work on the justice system with the question: 'What's wrong with the justice system in Britain today?' Answers would be patchy and lacking in any depth of knowledge. Instead, save your open questions until after students are secure in the key factual knowledge. You will stimulate a much more insightful discussion if you do.

♦ **Attempting to engage a poorly behaved or unfocused class through discussion.** If your class are unwilling to behave well, then cut out questioning and discussion as much as possible. Contrary to popular belief, it is very hard to solve behaviour issues by trying to make your lessons more interactive. It tends to backfire because discussions give further opportunity for mischief-makers to play up to their peers. Once you have re-established calm and respect, you can slowly introduce short, structured opportunities for debate and talk.

Should I be mindful about how long my class spend questioning and discussing?

Yes. Quite how long a discussion should last is similar to the proverbial 'how long is a piece of string?' Remember that even though you will feel very involved in the discussion as a teacher, there could be plenty of students who have stopped attending. During discussion only one person is speaking; during independent work every child is compelled to think for themselves. And don't forget the importance of practice. If your discussions are dragging on you will be cutting into practice time. It is natural to feel guilty that you cannot hear from every student in the lesson, but that is the nature of thirty-to-a-class teaching. Stick to your guns and keep discussion sharp and focused.

How do I manage the extrovert/introvert divide?

About one-third to one-half of your students are likely to be introverts.[9] Classrooms are designed for the personalities of

---

9   See Susan Cain, *Quiet: The Power of Introverts in a World That Can't Stop Talking* (London: Penguin, 2012), pp. 3–4.

extroverted children, who are quite happy to participate noisily, sociably and enthusiastically in dialogue. Introverts, on the other hand, are quieter and need more time to reflect. This does not mean that you let some children choose not to participate; it just means that you need to be mindful that not all will reveal their true colours when put on the spot in front of their classmates.

The most important thing you can do is to give all children an ample amount of time to think before they share ideas – that is, remember to pause. When they do share, ensure that the ideas of introverts are given equal weight to those of extroverts. Focus on what they say, not how they say it. Finally, never write in a school report, 'They need to speak up more in class.' This is a comment about the child's personality, not necessarily their capability in your subject. If anything, it could send the child further into their shell.

Chapter 7
Embedding the Ethos

So far in this book we have looked at how adopting six ped-agogical principles can enable us to embed two core values in our teaching. The first was excellence, the idea that we should encourage our students not to be satisfied with medi-ocrity, but to refine, redraft and hone their work towards a higher goal. The second was growth, the notion that intelli-gence and achievement are not fixed. Through hard work, effort, resilience and determination we can all get better at what we do.

While the implementation of these pedagogical principles will go a long way to embed the ethos of excellence and growth, there are many other factors that define a school's culture. For example:

- Assessing and monitoring the quality of teaching.
- Continuing professional development.
- Assessment, target-setting and reports.
- Curriculum planning.
- Assemblies and form time.
- The physical environment.
- Behaviour and behaviour policy.

If we really want to shape the culture of our schools, these values must permeate everything we do. This final chapter aims to encourage school leaders and teachers to reflect on how the values of excellence and growth should drive all key decisions within a school, not just those made by individual teachers behind closed doors. To help you to reflect on how you might do this, we will present some general principles along with a number of practical case studies from schools across the country, including our own.

Assessing and Monitoring the Quality of Teaching in Schools

It is no surprise that the most effective schools have a relentless focus on improving the quality of teaching. To do this, we need to know what works and what does not, and then reduce any variation in the quality of practice. This is what good school leaders should be doing. Where this has gone wrong, though, is the way in which it has been undertaken.

It has become standard practice in schools to observe teachers a few times a year. These observations may be whole lessons, yet are often only for part of the lesson – sometimes only thirty minutes. Then, after each observation, we make a judgement on the teacher, based on Ofsted criteria. They will be either outstanding, good, requires improvement or inadequate.

This is a less than useful situation for a number of reasons. First, in that same way that students just look at a grade and largely ignore any formative feedback (if given both), human nature will work in the same way with adults. If given a grade for our teaching, we will tend to focus on that and ignore the formative feedback. Second, the Ofsted quality of teaching judgement criteria were never meant to be used for individual lessons. Instead, they were supposed to be used to make an overall judgement about the quality of teaching in a school. Finally, and most importantly, how can we possibly make a judgement about a teacher based on such a small sample of what they do? The answer is we can't. It would be like judging Pelé as an inadequate footballer because of the chance he missed against Uruguay in the 1970 World Cup semi-final, while ignoring the stunning 1,281 goals he scored in his otherwise remarkable career!

Lesson observation ought to be used in a formative way to support teacher development. It should be a professional dialogue between the observer and the observee that supports reflection and professional growth – for both. To do this we must stop grading lessons and steer clear of any tick-list approach to lesson observation: there should be no prescribed way of teaching. Teachers should not be criticised because their style of teaching does not fit into somebody else's model of a good lesson – as long as it's working, of course, and students are attaining.

A far more sensible approach is to observe lessons with a blank sheet of paper, note down what is happening during the lesson and then have a discussion afterwards about what the teacher was trying to do and how the students responded. This should then lead on quite naturally to a discussion about how adjustments could be made to the teaching with a view to making it even more effective. By taking away the element of judgement, the observer becomes a critical friend and the teacher, significantly, takes ownership of the improvement process.

The other issue is the assumption that the only way to make a judgement about teacher effectiveness is through lesson observation. Teaching is a multifaceted job. There are many things that teachers do which will ultimately determine how students perform in examinations. They teach lessons, they mark books and assessments, they meet parents, they set homework, they give written feedback, they give verbal feedback, they help with revision, they support, they encourage and they inspire. All of these things should be taken into account when making a judgement about teacher effectiveness.

As teachers and leaders, if we are going to make an accurate judgement about ourselves, we are all 'requires improvement'. Because there is no such thing as perfect. We can all get that little bit better, all of the time. As leaders and colleagues, our job is to support and facilitate that process.

As Dylan Wiliam says, 'Every teacher needs to improve, not because they are not good enough, but because they can be even better.'[1]

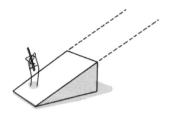

Continuing Professional Development

All great schools have something in common. They are filled to the brim with enthusiastic teachers who enjoy talking about teaching, sharing ideas and trying things out. Similarly, they will have leaders who facilitate and encourage this. It is not a complicated idea, but it does require a shift in how we think about the leadership of teaching and learning/CPD in schools. In the same way that we want our students to strive for excellence, we should look to foster the same kind of culture with our staff. The following points are worth consideration by school leaders.

---

1 Dylan Wiliam, Keynote speech at the SSAT National Conference, Liverpool, December 2012.

Find the Bright Spots

In their book, *Switch: How to Change Things When Change Is Hard*, Chip and Dan Heath describe what successful institutions do: they find what is working and do more of it – they 'find the bright spots'.[2] A change has more likelihood of taking root if it comes from within rather than if it is imposed from the outside. Do this in your school. Find the teachers who are employing successful strategies in their classrooms and use them to lead CPD for other teachers. There are a range of CPD strategies that do this, like weekly staff-led fifteen-minute forums for instance. Ideas such as these can be further explored in Shaun's book, *Perfect Teacher-Led CPD*.[3] You have a huge number of experts in the classrooms of your school. Use them!

Look Outside

Use the experts within your school to develop teaching, but do not forget to look outside too. A growing number of teachers are sharing their thoughts and practice through social media, such as Twitter and education blogs. Alongside this, it is now easier than ever before to access educational research papers and books that highlight successful teaching practice from across the world. Many schools are creating new 'research lead' roles to support their staff to become 'research aware' and then 'research engaged'.

Do you know what research evidence has revealed about the areas you need to improve at your school? Do you know what educational research is being carried out by your local university, and could you work alongside them? Is there a TeachMeet happening locally that your staff could choose to

---

2 Chip Heath and Dan Heath, *Switch: How to Change Things When Change Is Hard* (London: Random House, 2011).
3 Shaun Allison, *Perfect Teacher-Led CPD* (Carmarthen: Independent Thinking Press, 2014).

attend? If not, could you host one? These are all excellent CPD avenues that should be explored and positively embraced. However, make sure you use these approaches to enhance the wisdom you already have in your school, and whenever possible give staff the choice about whether they would like to opt in. Rigid imposition will most likely lead to resistance and frustration.

Take a Layered Approach to CPD

As a school, do you ensure that there is a variety of CPD activities open to staff that allow them to access CPD at a level that suits them? Especially important are collaborative CPD activities such as lesson study and coaching, as they encourage teachers to learn from and support each other (as in the example below):

A layered approach to CPD
Blanket Important developmental work that all teachers need to be involved in – that aligns with whole-school improvement priorities. *Delivered through: INSET days/staff meetings/ appraisal etc.*
Optional A range of developmental activities that teachers can opt in to, with a view to personalising their CPD and so allowing them to follow their own interests. *Delivered through: 15-minute forums, IRIS observations, lesson study, peer observations, action research, coaching, school visits etc.*

Directed

When staff are underperforming they are directed to engage in specific developmental/support work.

Delivered through: Mentoring/coaching

We need to create the right climate in schools – one that is supportive, collaborative and encourages teachers to explore, challenge themselves and grow. A fresh look at CPD is needed by school leaders. This requires schools to develop a bottom-up, teacher-led approach to CPD as opposed to a top-down, one-size-fits-all approach. For too long, teachers have been shackled by unfortunate fads and gimmicks telling them how they should be teaching. This has disempowered and demoralised large sections of the profession. The challenge for us as educators, then, is to seize back our profession. We need to let teachers teach, make them excited about teaching and learn from each other.

In the final section of this chapter, we will present case studies focusing on three main areas: assessment, target-setting and reports; the curriculum; and behaviour.

Assessment, Target-Setting and Reports

Case Study: Durrington High School, West Sussex

In May 2014, Durrington High School was awarded an Assessment Innovation Fund by the Department for Education to develop a method of 'assessing without levels' in Key Stage 3. We developed a 'growth and thresholds' method of assessment in line with our principles of growth and excellence across the school. A set of principles guided the assessment model. We aimed to develop an assessment system based on:

♦ Developing key knowledge and skills required for success in Key Stage 4.

♦ High expected standards of students.

♦ Formative feedback that allows all students to succeed – and so develops a growth mindset.

♦ Periodic summative assessment to support ongoing formative feedback.

♦ Simple and easy to understand guidelines for staff, parents and students.

♦ Consistent principles but with the flexibility to be suitable for all subjects.

The Growth and Thresholds Model in a Nutshell

Subject specialist teachers come up with the 'big ideas' in their subject – the key concepts crucial to mastery in that subject. From this, they consider the question: in terms of knowledge and skills, what do students need to master to be successful at Key Stage 4? Based on this, they decide what excellence looks like in each subject. Starting from a baseline threshold, they then scaffold students towards excellence through the thresholds by giving them feedback about how to progress to the next one. The thresholds are used to plan for progression and to focus assessment and feedback on the key knowledge and skills.

Implementation

Use Key Stage 2 Levels to Place Students into 'Thresholds'

Key Stage 2 levels are used to place students into four ability bands (thresholds – as in the example below) linked to future GCSE grades. These thresholds are not 'labels' for students and the students are not told them. They are a planning tool for teachers. When used in conjunction with the threshold rubrics, they give a starting point to plan for progression.

KS2 Levels	KS3 Thresholds	GCSE (Current)	GCSE (New)
5a+	Excellence	A*	9-8
5	Secure	A-B	7-6
4	Developing	B-C	5-4
3-2	Foundation	D-G	3-1

Subject Areas Identify the Core Knowledge and Skills

The starting point is for each subject area to identify the core knowledge and skills that students will need to master in order to be successful at GCSE. This will be based on the knowledge and skills that subject staff know to be key to success in Years 10 and 11, linked to the national curriculum programme of study. For example, in science the core knowledge might be: cells, interdependence, forces, energy and particles, and the core skills might be: identify, describe, explain, analyse and link. Once we know where we want the students to go in our subjects, we can then use this to plan the curriculum backwards from Years 7–11.

Subject Areas Outline the Standard Expected from Each Threshold

Once subject areas have this starting point, they can then start to map out the curriculum across Years 7–11. This involves looking at what the big ideas are, what topics will be taught and when and what key knowledge and skills will be assessed in each unit of work.

For each unit of work, subject teachers discuss, decide and agree the standards expected from each threshold, in terms of the core knowledge and skills. This allows them to set the high standards expected from students – a key principle of the model of assessment. It also allows them to be selective about the key knowledge and skills that are important and so need to be assessed. They do not just evaluate everything – they focus on and assess what matters.

Each unit of work starts with a completed copy of this threshold rubric – what is expected within that unit of work in terms of knowledge and skills, at each of the four thresholds. This, when used with student baseline thresholds, allows teachers to plan for progression within their teaching.

Threshold	Threshold knowledge	Threshold skills
Excellence		
Secure		
Developing		
Foundation		

Thresholds could be based around SOLO taxonomy. Foundation and developing are aimed at surface learning (i.e. embedding the key knowledge/facts). Secure and excellence are more focused on developing deep learning (doing something with this key knowledge, e.g. analysis, linking ideas, evaluation). It is important to note that while SOLO might provide a good framework for planning learning in some subjects, it might not be suitable for all subjects. This leads to the production of a learning schedule for that unit of work where the key knowledge and skills to be learnt are broken down into individual lessons.

Ensuring Progression

When subjects plan their thresholds, there has to be progression through the years. For example, if a student has a baseline threshold of 'developing', making expected progress through Key Stage 3 indicates that they should achieve a minimum of a grade C by the end of Year 11. This means that the 'developing' thresholds in Years 7, 8 and 9 should show increasing levels of demand in terms of expectation to allow them to maintain this trajectory. Ideally, they would rise through the thresholds towards 'excellence'.

Tracking Progress and Reporting to Parents

In tracking progress and reporting to parents, performance is considered relative to baseline threshold:

- ◆ Working below their baseline threshold = less than expected progress.

- ◆ Working towards the lower end of their baseline threshold = expected progress.

- ◆ Working towards the top end of their baseline threshold = good progress.

- ◆ Working above their baseline threshold or at the top of or beyond the excellence threshold = exceptional progress.

Departments devise suitable assessment tasks that allow them to assess, against the thresholds, periodically through the year. In addition, a scoring system records this progress quantitatively in spreadsheets, SIMS (School Information Management System) and so on. This is just for internal analysis and is not shared with parents or students.

Formative Assessment

The banded thresholds of knowledge and skills can then be used to give students ongoing and personalised formative feedback on their day-to-day work, focusing on how to improve towards excellence. In order to support a growth mindset, the feedback is aimed at moving students through the thresholds so that they aspire towards excellence and develop resilience and grit. This keeps expectations consistently high, and it is why the rubrics are an essential planning tool.

Summative Assessment

Summative assessments (termly) are used to further assess how well students are doing towards the end of the unit of work. Their performance on these tests can be used to measure their progress against their baseline threshold.

How Is It Different from Levels?

♦ Students are not assigned a target level; they are all expected to aspire to excellence.

♦ Assessment is based on progress made, celebrating the effort of all students whatever their starting points.

♦ Teachers set the standard of excellence expected, not an outside body.

♦ Students are not given feedback such as 'you're a 4a' , but formative feedback that makes students think about how to develop their understanding.

♦ Rubrics are used for planning teaching and progression, not assigning numbers.

Curriculum and Beyond

Case Study: Belmont Community School, Durham

Key Influences

Much of our recent work in school has been strongly influenced by the work of Ron Berger, the chief programme officer for Expeditionary Learning, such as *An Ethic of Excellence* and *Leaders of Their Own Learning*,[4] as well as professor of psychology at Stanford University, Carol Dweck's books *Self-Theories* and *Mindset*.[5]

All of our staff – teaching staff, support staff and governors – have been given wide access and exposure to this work in school. We have multiple copies of these books in our teaching and learning library, where they top our loan statistics by some margin. All of our learning hub leaders have a personal copy, as well as those who have elected to read them in their Edu-Book Club as part of their personal professional development programme. This is supported by a compendium of blogs and videos we have compiled and continue to update on excellence and mindset.

---

4 Berger, *An Ethic of Excellence*; Ron Berger, Leah Rugen and Libby Woodfin, *Leaders of Their Own Learning: Transforming Schools Through Student-Engaged Assessment* (San Francisco, CA: Jossey-Bass, 2014).

5 Carol Dweck, *Self-Theories: Their Role in Motivation, Personality, and Development* (Essays in Social Psychology) (Philadelphia, PA: Psychology Press, 2000); Carol Dweck, *Mindset: The New Psychology of Success* (New York: Ballantine, 2007).

Learning Hubs

To further ensure we develop an ethic of excellence and growth mindset among our learning community, all members of our teaching staff work in a choice of one of five learning hubs as part of their personal professional development programme.

Our learning hubs operate along the lines of Dylan Wiliam's teacher learning communities (TLCs) model, with each hub, comprising approximately eight to twelve staff meeting for two hours once every half-term, with the following aims:

- **Challenge**
  - ◊ To embed a culture of growth mindset across our learning community in order to raise aspirations and expectations of what students can achieve.
  - ◊ To ensure high levels of challenge for all students in every lesson, every day.

- **E-learning**
  - ◊ To use e-learning to embed a culture of growth mindset by empowering students, staff and parents to become engaged, confident, independent, resilient, information-literate users of e-learning.
  - ◊ To develop personalised e-learning resources for staff (teaching/pedagogy), students (learning) and parents (to support learning process as active participants).

- **Feedback and critique**
  - ◊ To consider the nature, timing and engagement of our students with feedback and critique.
  - ◊ To develop feedback and critique systems that ensure increased clarity, effort and aspiration among our students, supporting a culture of growth mindset.

♦ **Literacy**

◊ To consider how the language of subject specialisms can be explicitly taught by all teachers and supported by parents through a range of strategies.

◊ To develop students' chances of academic success by insisting that academic language is used in the classroom, and at home when talking to parents about schoolwork.

♦ **Questioning**

◊ To develop deep and probing questioning for teaching/memory that elicits students to think hard, supporting a culture of growth mindset and questioning for assessment that informs teaching, such as hinge questions, multiple-choice quizzing, etc.

Mindset Across the Curriculum

Our mindset work forms not only part of our pastoral programme, but it is also supported by subject areas in lessons around five key themes: motivation and inspirations, aspirations, resilience, self-esteem and mindset. All students complete a learning journal during tutor-time as part of this work.

A Golden Opportunity

The abolition of levels at Key Stage 3 provided us with an ideal opportunity to create not just a new assessment system, but an entire curriculum based on the principles of excellence and growth. Central to this was the idea that everyone is capable of excellence.

The curriculum we have created is a curriculum *we* value – a curriculum designed to focus on fewer things in greater depth, rather than being inch deep and mile wide. To achieve this we have invested in regular blocks of time for our staff so that they can work together in teams to design subject-specific curriculum and assessment.

Key Components

Each subject started by establishing their organising concepts, or 'big ideas', which required a review of the entire national curriculum from Key Stages 1–4. Knowing the prior learning of our students enabled us to accelerate from it and ensure high challenge from the outset. It also allowed us to introduce GCSE knowledge and skills in Years 7–9 and go beyond the typical confines for the year or key stage.

We've also been very careful to pay attention to what cognitive science tells us about learning and memory, embracing the work of UCLA psychology professor Robert A. Bjork. As a consequence, organising concepts are spaced and interleaved in order to try to build greater storage and retrieval strength. In doing this, we hope to be able to challenge our students further by increasing their knowledge base and recall. This frees up working memory to allow them to think hard about and assimilate new information.

Assessment is then focused on mastery of fundamental concepts, ideas, knowledge and skills by designing rubrics containing learning targets for each unit ranging from 'establishing' at a basic understanding through to the highest thresholds of 'excellence' and 'beyond'. As part of our commitment to excellence and growth, we believe that futures aren't fixed and that all students have the potential for excellence and can improve by working hard and putting in their very best effort, acting on feedback from their teachers and becoming leaders of their own learning. As part of this commitment, all students are given access and the opportunity to demonstrate their learning right up to the 'beyond' threshold.

As well as specifying information about lesson resources, homework and assessment opportunities, each unit also contains a link to previous interleaved sequences, as well as deep and probing questions which are designed in advance to encourage students to think hard about new information. As professor of psychology Daniel Willingham says, 'Memory is the residue of thought'[6] or as Durham University professor Robert Coe puts it, 'Learning happens when people have to think hard.'[7]

Assessment, Recording and Reporting

In a similar fashion, our assessment, recording and reporting of student progress has been revised to incorporate our philosophy of excellence and growth. MidYIS testing on entry is used to identify any potential that may have been missed previously. Progress is reported relative to starting points in simple terms as 'excellent', 'good' or 'not yet' – incorporating the language of growth. The bar is set high, so that meeting your baseline threshold represents good progress from the starting point in each unit. In a similar way, our revised descriptors for effort encourage excellence and growth. For effort to be classed as excellent, for example, a student must:

♦ Consistently strive for excellence.

♦ Take ownership of their own learning.

♦ Be highly organised and self-disciplined.

♦ Show initiative and responsibility.

♦ Show real determination in pursuit of goals.

♦ Demonstrate resilience when things get hard.

♦ Continuously seek, reflect and act on all feedback.

♦ Actively participate and contribute for the benefit of all.

This year, in our efforts to help our students become leaders of their own learning, we have replaced our traditional

---

6   Willingham, *Why Don't Students Like School?*, p. 54.
7   Robert Coe, *Improving Education: A Triumph of Hope over Experience*, Inaugural Lecture of Professor Robert Coe, Durham University, 18 June 2013, xiii.

annual report with a series of student-led conferences in each subject area. These give students an opportunity to share their work and talk about their progress with parents and teachers by reflecting on and articulating what they have learnt.

REAL Projects and realsmart

Recently, we've been working with realsmart to try to support the learning process even further by giving our students the opportunity to submit evidence of meeting learning targets to their cloud-based learning portfolios. Any evidence submitted can then be used as a starting point to discuss progress at their student-led conferences.

We've also started working with a Project-Based Learning coach from High Tech High in San Diego, through the Innovation Unit, to develop REAL (rigorous, engaging, authentic, learning) projects whose three key principles support our philosophy of excellence and growth:

1   All students are capable of excellence, regardless of prior attainment, needs or background.

2   Student work should matter.

3   Schools and classrooms are communities of learners.

Through this work, our staff and students are being trained to build a culture of peer feedback, critique and multiple drafting through the use of models of excellence. These skills are further developed during our whole-school project week in the summer term which involves public exhibition of high quality student work. Our Ethic of Excellence gallery, which sits in the heart of our school, also complements this by displaying beautiful student work nominated by individual subjects.

Dan Brinton, deputy head teacher
(read more on Dan's blog at https://belmontteach.wordpress.com/
and follow Dan on Twitter @dan_brinton)

Assemblies and Form Time

Case Study: Chew Valley School, Somerset

At Chew Valley School, a rural comprehensive in north-east Somerset, we launched a new ethos, mission and set of aims in September 2014: to develop a growth mindset in all members of the school. The launch was a full year in the planning, addressing staff development, parental engagement, feedback, reporting, assessment and behaviour. The core business, however, was to get students to understand the principles of a growth mindset and ways they could begin to shift their own approach to work, practice and learning. The best vehicle to reach them as consistently as possible was through the twin vehicles of assemblies and tutor sessions.

The launch assembly was the cornerstone of the approach. How best to communicate growth mindset in fifteen minutes? I didn't want to overcomplicate it, so I began by thinking about the most important information that students needed to know. I came up with:

♦ The difference between a growth and fixed mindset.

♦ The basic neuroscience of how the brain learns.

♦ How this neuroscience can be used to understand the benefits of a growth mindset.

♦ How to use a growth mindset voice in learning situations.

The key part of the assembly was emphasising why the growth mindset attributes – embracing challenges, seeing effort as the path to mastery, learning from critique and the success of others – help to develop intelligence by growing and developing neural pathways. Struggle is essential for learning. I also made sure that the students knew that all the teachers were working hard to develop a growth mindset in teaching and learning teams to ensure that the quality of teaching continued to be excellent and improving. It was important that students understood that learning, growth and achievement are critical for every member of the school community.

The themes from the launch assembly were picked up by tutors in the following week in a whole-school tutorial session. This session used 'The Learning Brain' video to reinforce the principles of neuroscience from the assembly.[8] This was followed up with a choice of activities including questions about scenarios, individual effort stories or practical tasks to demonstrate the benefit of practice and repetition.

Of course, the launch assembly was just the beginning; critical to the success of our new approach was embedding it in daily practice. Ongoing assemblies throughout the year reflected six themes – growth, effort, resilience, deliberate practice, grit and reflection – one for each term. The responsibility for delivering these themes was divided across senior and middle leaders in the school so that students could see it was a shared, coherent message. Tutors continued their input by picking up on assembly threads in their daily interactions with students. They also asked students to reflect each week on their approach to learning in the previous week, setting targets for improvement and development in learning reflection journals. At each reporting point, students have completed more detailed reflections on their progress over time and the way in which their approach to learning has influenced their attainment.

The impact has been noticeable. The school *feels* different, and there is a unity of approach among staff in their interactions with young people. Our evaluations of attitudes to learning within Year 11 show that they are consistently higher than with any year group since we began collecting

---

8   See: https://www.youtube.com/watch?v=cgLYkV689s4.

this data. We are only at the beginning of our journey, but we feel like we're on the right path.

Chris Hildrew, deputy head teacher
(read more on Chris' blog at https://chrishildrew.wordpress.com/
and follow Chris on Twitter @chrishildrew)

Physical Environment

Case Study: Les Quennevais School, Jersey

I have spoken to a few seasoned Ofsted inspectors who have commented that they can get a feel for a school, what it stands for and the expectations of their students, from their first few steps into the building. The corridors, the walls, the very fabric of the building should never be forgotten as part of your efforts to embed a culture of excellence and growth. The walls should exude what your school stands for, the aspirations you have for your students. Think of your walls as the skin that holds together the wonderful learning happening in your school. Every pore of that skin should breathe the culture you are trying to create.

As an art teacher, I have always made my art students feel like they are on a degree course, carefully framing their huge boards, lighting their work on crisp white walls with more than a nod to the parade of top-end galleries in London's Cork Street. The only thing missing are the extortionate price tags. The reason we care so much is that many of these students have worked for fifty to a hundred hours on one painting. These students deserve the high quality recognition they receive, like L'Oréal, because they're worth it.

What about those subjects which are not quite as instantly beautiful as art, but where we still want to create a culture of excellence? This is why we decided to create our Ethic of Excellence wall. It's pretty huge for a small school: it spans half of the main corridor and was inspired by the Summer Exhibition display at the Royal Academy. There is a range of ornate frames which I got for free – up-cycled from a local framers, spruced up with brightly coloured spray paints and varnish and a simple black space where the picture would have been. It means we can quickly mount up a whole range of work which departments consider excellent; work which has been through the wringer of several drafts, many hours of improvement and commitment to being the best possible work that student has created.

Why wouldn't we want to make the most of sharing this excellence with the rest of the school and our community? Why on earth should all this hard work be graded, commented on and just placed back on the shelf? The work our students are capable of is extraordinary. Our wall of excellence is just one example of how we are getting everyone who learns at our school, and I include our teachers in this too, to recognise that brilliant geography essay on the Serengeti, that wonderful model of healthy eating created for a food tech homework, that exquisite poem about the Battle of the Somme. It needs to be seen, doesn't it?

A big part of having a growth mindset is being inspired by the greatness of others. For this to happen, we all need to think about how we do this. Our wall of excellence has been a huge hit with our students and our community. People who visit the school always comment on what a wonderful way it is to display the work of our students. It has inspired so many students to 'get their finger out' and try their hardest for this recognition.

I started this process by asking the students what excellence meant to them, following a whole-school assembly launch of the idea. The students' responses just blew me away. I managed to fill every frame with inspiring quotes; not from famous dead white scientists, but from the living greats who walk through our doors every day – our students. So inspiring were these quotes that they now hang around the school permanently. It really hit me. These kids are here for the taking – look at their expectations of what excellence is. They really get it. They deserve a curriculum that is all about excellence. They need the opportunity to understand and create their own excellence, and they need the opportunity to share their excellence with others. A simple idea, but one which has gone a long way in developing a culture of excellence at our school.

'If you don't make it first time, just keep trying. You will get there eventually and be really happy with all the work you have put in.'

For students, the wall of excellence has clearly helped to embody the culture we are aiming to create in our school. For example, students in Year 11 who previously were never bothered about working 'above and beyond' have told me that they are determined to get their work on the wall before they leave. Fingers point with immense pride by those who see their work, and equally inspire others to think about what they need to do to achieve similar greatness. Parents have taken photos of their child in front of their work on the wall, with both generations developing their understanding of the ethos we are building.

The fact that such care and respect is given to students' work of excellence from all subjects tells the students at Les Quennevais School a great deal about the culture we are aiming to surround them with. The wall is looked at every single day by many staff and students and serves as a powerful reminder of what excellence looks like. Staff are also thinking of the design of their curriculum and how they can ensure more and more students are able to create work of excellence.

Pete Jones, assistant head teacher (read more on Pete's blog http:// deeplearning.edublogs.org/ and follow Pete on Twitter @Pekabelo)

Behaviour

Case Study: Durrington High School, West Sussex

What Does 'Growth Mindset' Mean to Me?

In the context of my role as whole-school behaviour leader, growth mindset is primarily about holding the belief that the behaviour schools and teachers see from a student is only an output of a mixture of environmental factors and experiences within the child's life; in short, no student is born bad. So, in the same way that we believe all students can improve their academic performance with sustained effort and hard work, we also believe that students who are getting their behaviour wrong can change and get it right.

This deeper understanding of the individual's behaviour, when seeing them day in, day out, is the foundation stone on which I believe the school has seen a rapid and sustained improvement in nearly all student behaviour measures over the last two years. These have included the number of fixed-term exclusions falling substantially and a sustained reduction in incidents of poor behaviour. We are not there yet, but we will be soon!

Growth Mindset in a Practical Sense

So much about working with challenging behaviour is getting the right support in place as quickly as possible – ideally in a preventative way – to address the behaviour of the individual at source. The growth mindset theory has made me more solution focused and has enabled me to accept the challenge, as a leader, to rapidly and consistently overcome the barriers faced by students who are making poor behavioural decisions. It has also reinforced my belief that every child can, and will, behave in a better way through our work and support in school – and, as a result, they will achieve better.

When working with staff, growth mindset has been about supporting them in becoming more resilient and consistent in the face of setbacks. 'Hope' and 'belief' have been consistent messages to the staff team I lead and work with, even in the most challenging of times. I am sure in some way that these messages and my personal refusal to believe that any child is beyond saving have helped them to recognise the positives as well as the negatives – that, in their own minds, they balance events and situations. These interactions have led to increased skill-sets and resilience as members of staff have learnt from each student case and, as a result, built considerable expertise in their fields of work.

I am not a great reader of education theory, but I know and truly believe – and the indicators demonstrate – that, as a result of my understanding and belief in the use of the principles of growth mindset, the school has improved dramatically. We are all emotionally stronger, more knowledgeable and, therefore, more effective in our roles.

Chris Woodcock, deputy head teacher

Summary

We remain convinced that fostering a culture of growth and excellence through great classroom teaching, as we've described in this book, is the right thing to do for our students. Not only is it grounded in evidence – in terms of what research tells us about how we learn and the principles of effective teaching – but it is also the right preparation for life beyond school. We are hoping to develop young people who understand that achievement in anything is grounded in hard work, effort and commitment to long-term goals. These are attributes that are essential not only for school but also for life beyond the school gates.

However, if you are committed to growth and excellence, it needs to be infused in everything you do as an educator, not only the lessons you teach. These principles should drive your curriculum, how you assess students, how you manage behaviour, how you lead your colleagues, how you interact with students and, indeed, how you construct the very fabric of your school building. Everything you do should exude the belief that, with the right attitude, there are very few limits to how the young people you serve can grow, flourish and achieve things that they once thought impossible.

Appendix 1
Index of Strategies

Chapter 3: Modelling

Chapter 4: Practice

Appendix 2

Planning and Reflection Tool

This tool can be used by teachers to reflect on their own practice and then inform their lesson planning.

Challenge

- Are learning objectives single and challenging for all?
- Are all students expected to develop their knowledge and skills during the lesson?
- Is formal, subject-specific, academic language modelled by teachers and encouraged from students?
- Is the bar of expectation high for all students?
- Is appropriate support and scaffolding in place to enable all students to achieve this level of expectation?
- Are examples of excellence shared, discussed and deconstructed with the class?
- Is subject content relevant and challenging?
- Are assessment criteria referred to explicitly?

Explanation

- Is prior knowledge established and used to 'hook into' new knowledge?
- Does the explanation focus on the key learning points, success criteria and subject threshold concepts?
- Are there opportunities to make the explanation more concrete and credible e.g. demonstration, visual, practical, appropriate use of analogy, etc.?

- Does the explanation generate curiosity and so 'open up the learning gaps'?

- Is explanation clear and concise, especially when subject matter is challenging?

- Is teacher talk and gesture enthusiastic, kind and inclusive?

Modelling

- Is practical work and other activities carefully modelled?

- Are examples of excellent work shared and compared? 'This is great because…'

- Are exemplary examples of subject-specific products, including writing, deconstructed with the students?

- Is subject-specific writing then modelled and co-constructed with the students?

- Does teaching allow critique of models?

- Is 'expert thinking' modelled by verbalising implicit thought processes?

- Is modelling scaffolded to maximise the learning for all students?

Practice

- Once students have had input from the teacher, are they given time to practise the new knowledge and skills?

- Are mistakes observed, leading to intervention when necessary to ensure that practice is perfect?

- Are mistakes utilised as a key aspect of leaning?

- Is practice supported by scaffolds and support when necessary?

- Are scaffolds and supports removed at the right time to allow for independence?

♦ Is there evidence that threshold concepts (key subject-specific knowledge and skills) are practised regularly to improve retention?

Feedback

♦ Is there a good mix of verbal and written feedback?

♦ Are students encouraged to critique the work of their peers?

♦ Is feedback kind, specific and helpful?

♦ Is feedback designed to make students think – instead of giving them the answer?

♦ Is feedback timed right i.e. are students given enough 'struggle time'?

♦ Are students expected to move towards 'closing the gap' by responding to feedback?

♦ As a result, do students know what they have got to do to achieve?

♦ Are self-assessment strategies such as proofreading, editing and redrafting employed to aid metacognition?

♦ Is teaching flexible, based on feedback from the performance of students?

Questioning

♦ Does questioning involve a wide range of students?

♦ Does questioning both deepen and develop thinking and check for common misconceptions?

♦ Are student responses developed by further questioning?

♦ Are reluctant respondents encouraged to respond by careful scaffolding?

♦ Are students encouraged to respond to and evaluate the responses of their peers?

- Are students encouraged to ask questions?
- Are students expected to rephrase answers in Standard English?

Bibliography

Allison, Shaun (2014). *Perfect Teacher-Led CPD* (Carmarthen: Independent Thinking Press).

Bandura, Albert (1977). Self-Efficacy: Towards a Unifying Theory of Behaviour Change, *Psychological Review* 84(2): 191–215. Available at: http://www.uky.edu/~eushe2/Bandura/Bandura1977PR.pdf.

Beere, Jackie (2010). *The Perfect Ofsted Lesson* (Carmarthen: Crown House Publishing).

Berger, Ron (2003). *An Ethic of Excellence: Building a Culture of Craftsmanship with Students* (Portsmouth, NH: Heinemann).

Berger, Ron, Leah Rugen and Libby Woodfin (2014). *Leaders of Their Own Learning: Transforming Schools Through Student-Engaged Assessment* (San Francisco, CA: Jossey-Bass).

Biggs, John and Kevin Collis (1982). *Evaluating the Quality of Learning: The SOLO Taxonomy* (New York: Academic Press).

Brown, Peter C., Henry L. Roediger III and Mark A. McDaniel (2014). *Make It Stick: The Science of Successful Learning* (Cambridge, MA: Harvard University Press).

Cain, Susan (2012). *Quiet: The Power of Introverts in a World That Can't Stop Talking* (London: Penguin).

Carey, Benedict (2014). *How We Learn: The Surprising Truth About When, Where and Why It Happens* [Kindle edn] (London: Macmillan).

Coe, Robert (2013). *Improving Education: A Triumph of Hope over Experience*, Inaugural Lecture of Professor Robert Coe, Durham University, 18 June.

Coe, Robert, Cesare Aloisi, Steve Higgins and Lee Elliot Major (2014). *What Makes Great Teaching? Review of the Underpinning Research* (London: Sutton Trust). Available at: http://www.suttontrust.com/wp-content/uploads/2014/10/What-makes-great-teaching-FINAL-4.11.14.pdf.

Curtis, Chris (2015). Marking – The Circles of Correction, *Learning from My Mistakes: An English Teacher's Blog* (8 March). Available at: http://learningfrommymistakesenglish.blogspot.co.uk/2015/03/marking-circles-of-correction.html.

Day, Andy (2014). Questioning for Deliberation: TLT14 Session Summary, *Meridianvale* (27 October). Available at: https://meridianvale.wordpress.com/2014/10/27/questioning-for-deliberation-tlt14-session-summary/.

Didau, David (2012). Slow Writing: How Slowing Down Can Improve Your Writing, *The Learning Spy* (12 May). Available at: http://www.learningspy.co.uk/english-gcse/how-to-improve-writing/.

Didau, David (2014). Getting Feedback Right Part 2: How Do We Provide Clarity?, *The Learning Spy* (5 March). Available at: http://www.learningspy.co.uk/assessment/getting-feedback-right-part-2-provide-clarity/.

Didau, David (2014). *The Secret of Literacy: Making the Implicit Explicit* (Carmarthen: Independent Thinking Press).

Dunlosky, John, Katherine A. Rawson, Elizabeth J. Marsh, Mitchell J. Nathan and Daniel T. Willingham (2013). Improving Students' Learning with Effective Learning Techniques: Promising Directions from Cognitive and Educational Psychology, *Psychological Science in the Public Interest* 14(1): 4–58. Available at: http://www.indiana.edu/~pcl/rgoldsto/courses/dunloskyimprovinglearning.pdf.

Dweck, Carol (2000). *Self-Theories: Their Role in Motivation, Personality, and Development* (Essays in Social Psychology) (Philadelphia, PA: Psychology Press).

Dweck, Carol (2007). *Mindset: The New Psychology of Success* (New York: Ballantine).

Ericsson, K. Anders, Ralf Th. Krampe and Clemens Tesch-Romer (1993). The Role of Deliberate Practice in the Acquisition of Expert Performance, *Psychological Review* 100(3): 363–406. Available at: http://graphics8.nytimes.com/images/blogs/freakonomics/pdf/DeliberatePractice%28PsychologicalReview%29.pdf.

Gallagher, Kelly (2011). *Write Like This: Teaching Real-World Writing Through Modelling and Mentor Texts* (Portland, ME: Stenhouse Publishers).

Gladwell, Malcolm (2008). *Outliers: The Story of Success* (London: Penguin).

Harrison, Allan G. and Richard K. Coll (eds) (2008). *Using Analogies in Middle and Secondary Science Classrooms: The FAR Guide – An Interesting Way to Teach with Analogies* (Thousand Oaks, CA: Corwin).

Hattie, John (2009). *Visible Learning: A Synthesis of Over 800 Meta-Analyses Relating to Achievement* (New York: Routledge).

Hattie, John (2014). The Science of Learning. Keynote speech presented at OSIRIS World-Class Schools Convention, London.

Hattie, John and Helen Timperley (2007). The Power of Feedback, *Review of Educational Research* 77(1): 81–112. Available at: http://education.qld.gov.au/staff/development/performance/resources/readings/power-feedback.pdf.

Hattie, John and Gregory Yates (2014). *Visible Learning and the Science of How We Learn* (Abingdon: Routledge).

Heath, Chip and Dan Heath (2007). *Made to Stick: Why Some Ideas Take Hold and Others Come Unstuck* (London: Arrow Books).

Heath, Chip and Dan Heath (2011). *Switch: How to Change Things When Change Is Hard* (London: Random House).

Kahneman, Daniel (2011). *Thinking, Fast and Slow* [Kindle edn] (London: Allen Lane).

Kirschner, Paul A., John Sweller and Richard E. Clark (2006). Why Minimal Guidance During Instruction Does Not Work: An Analysis of the Failure of Constructivist, Discovery, Problem-Based, Experiential, and Inquiry-Based Teaching, *Educational Psychologist* 41(2): 75–86.

Lemov, Doug (2010). *Teach Like a Champion: 49 Techniques that Put Students on the Path to College* [Kindle edn] (San Francisco, CA: Jossey-Bass).

Lemov, Doug (2013). Has Anyone Tried a 'Dot Round'?, *Teach Like a Champion* (10 October). Available at: http://teachlikeachampion.com/blog/anyone-tried-dot-round/.

Lemov, Doug (2014). At First Glance: A Sentence Starter Adds Unexpected Rigor to Writing, *Teach Like a Champion* (13 January). Available at: http://teachlikeachampion.com/blog/first-glance-sentence-starter-adds-unexpected-rigor-writing/.

Lemov, Doug, Erica Woolway and Katie Yezzi (2012). *Practice Perfect: 42 Rules for Getting Better at Getting Better* (San Francisco, CA: Jossey-Bass).

Loewenstein, George (1994). The Psychology of Curiosity: A Review and Reinterpretation, *Psychological Bulletin* 116(1): 75–98. Available at: https://www.cmu.edu/dietrich/sds/docs/loewenstein/PsychofCuriosity.pdf.

Marland, Michael (1975). *The Craft of the Classroom: A Survival Guide* (Oxford: Heinemann Books).

Meyer, Jan H. and Ray Land (2003). Threshold Concepts and Troublesome Knowledge – Linkages to Ways of Thinking and Practising. In Chris Rust (ed.), *Improving Student Learning: Theory and Practice – Ten Years On* (Oxford: Oxford Centre for Staff and Learning Development), pp. 412–424.

Muijs, Daniel and David Reynolds (2011). *Effective Teaching: Evidence and Practice*, 3rd edn (London: Sage).

Nuthall, Graham (2007). *The Hidden Lives of Learners* (Wellington: New Zealand Council for Educational Research Press).

Oates, Tim (n.d.). Assessment Without Levels in Depth [video]. Available at: http://www.cambridgeassessment.org.uk/insights/assessment-without-levels-extended-version-tim-oates-insights/.

Quigley, Alex (2013). 'Disciplined Discussion' – As Easy as ABC, *Hunting English* (26 December). Available at: http://www.huntingenglish.com/2013/12/26/disciplined-discussion-easy-abc/.

Quigley, Alex (2014). *Teach Now! English: Becoming a Great English Teacher* [Kindle edn] (Abingdon: Routledge).

Rosenshine, Barak (2012). Principles of Instruction: Research-Based Strategies That All Teachers Should Know, *American Educator* 36(1): 12–19. Available at: https://www.aft.org/sites/default/files/periodicals/Rosenshine.pdf.

Rosenthal, Robert and Lenore Jacobson (1992). *Pygmalion in the Classroom* (Carmarthen: Crown House Publishing).

Shakeshaft, Nicholas G., Maciej Trzaskowski, Andrew McMillan, Kaili Rimfeld, Eva Krapohl, Claire M. A. Haworth, Philip S. Dale and Robert Plomin (2013). Strong Genetic Influence on a UK Nationwide Test of Educational Achievement at the End of Compulsory Education at Age 16, *PLoS ONE* 8(12): e80341. Available at: http://journals.plos.org/plosone/article?id=10.1371/journal.pone.0080341.

Soderstrom, Nicholas C. and Robert A. Bjork (2013). Learning versus Performance. In Dana Dunn (ed.), *Oxford Bibliographies Online: Psychology* (New York: Oxford University Press). Available at: http://bjorklab.psych.ucla.edu/pubs/Soderstrom_Bjork_Learning_versus_Performance.pdf.

Syed, Matthew (2011). *Bounce: The Myth of Talent and the Power of Practice* (London: Fourth Estate).

Wiliam, Dylan (2011). *Embedded Formative Assessment* [Kindle edn] (Bloomington, IN: Solution Tree Press).

Willingham, Daniel T. (2009). *Why Don't Students Like School? A Cognitive Scientist Answers Questions About How the Mind Works and What It Means for the Classroom* (San Francisco, CA: Jossey-Bass).

Young, Michael and David Lambert (2014). *Knowledge and the Future School: Curriculum and Social Justice* (London: Bloomsbury Academic).

Zimbardo, Philip (2011). The Pygmalion Effect and the Power of Positive Expectations [video] (25 September). Available at: http://www.youtube.com/watch?v=hTghEXKNj7g.

Index